KELLY'S KITCHEN SYNC

KELLY'S KITCHEN SYNC

Insider kitchen design and remodeling tips from an award–winning kitchen expert

Kelly Morisseau

Certified Master Kitchen Designer

SPRINGLINE
MEDIA

Kelly's Kitchen Sync

Author photography: Aimea Saul
Interior book design: David Moratto

ISBN 978-0-9828732-0-5

Springline Media

www.springlinemedia.com

ACKNOWLEDGMENTS

This book wouldn't have made it without the help, support and encouragement of home experts, clients, friends, fellow writers, and blog readers who generously offered their insights to make this book better.

In particular, I'd like to thank Jenni Gaynor, editor and reader, for her support and insight, Sharon Rowse, reader and fellow author, for her keen-eyed capture of garbled thoughts, Jen Ondrejka, friend and client, for her smarts and support (trust yourself — got it, sensei), Lisa Albert, reader and freelance writer, for her thoughts and enthusiasm for all things kitchens, and Scott Westby, second-generation general contractor, who patiently answered my questions of "Is this right?" and "What if...?

I'd also like to thank my consumer focus group, who generously gave of their time to make this book more of what they (and you) wanted to read, and the members of Blogger19 for their inspiration and support.

Lastly, I'd like to thank my mom, Carol Morisseau, CMKBD, CID, and my late father, Len Morisseau. If knowledge was a home, I've only updated the interiors. The solid foundation is all theirs.

TABLE OF CONTENTS

— PART 4 —

PUTTING IT ALL TOGETHER —

CASE STUDIES

For my mom, who always held the other end
of the tape measure so it didn't snap back,
and my dad, who always laughed when it did.

PART 1

EVERYONE NEEDS
A LITTLE DESIGN HELP—
THE EXPECTATIONS AND REALITY

CHAPTER 1

EVERYONE NEEDS A LITTLE DESIGN HELP

Ready to remodel your kitchen?

Great! It sounds so easy — buy a few cabinets, some appliances, and perhaps even replace a worn counter. Then you discover the dishwasher handle blocks a drawer, the refrigerator door hits the cabinets, and the dishwasher won't fit under the new counter.

Some of you may think you'll never run into this — after all, your kitchen is pretty simple without a lot of changes, right?

Here's the reality: designing the kitchen of today is like stacking dominoes. Every choice, every product, and every finish you add to your kitchen impacts the design, simple or not. One piece can send the rest tumbling if not thought out — and there are a lot of pieces!

I'm not trying to scare you, but rather provide a bit of hope — with the help of this book, you'll sail past all this. You'll learn how to spot those errors — and many others — long before you ever get to the installation stage.

This isn't a typical kitchen design book

I wrote this book for two reasons:

1. Most kitchen design books don't go beyond basic. By basic, I mean, you'll learn all about 'L'–shaped islands and the difference between gas or electric ranges. They don't mention how if you design two appliances at right angles into the corner of said 'L'-shaped kitchen, you won't ever be

able to open the corner cabinet. Or, if you have children under 5, purchasing the ultra–high–heat power of professional gas ranges might not be the safest idea for your family. That's what I wanted to tackle with this book.

2. Both my clients and my blog readers mentioned tales of woe by neighbors and on internet consumer forums, but it took all of them a bit of time to convince me. (What do I know? I don't get out of the showroom much!)

Although those of us in the design profession think there are thousands of us who specialize in kitchen design, my readers were letting me know by email that they couldn't find anyone.

So, here you go. If you're looking for insider information because you want to avoid the most common and expensive mistakes in kitchen design, this could be the book for you.

This is the second stage of design, the insider companion book that answers:
1) Who's out there and when do you need to hire them?
2) How to avoid the most common installation errors.
3) How French door refrigerators require different design techniques versus single–door refrigerators.
4) And more.

I'm a professional kitchen designer. The expertise in this book comes from over two decades of kitchen design experience, training, and yes, mistakes.

Meet your behind–the–scenes designer

My name is Kelly Morisseau, and I'm a Certified Master Kitchen and Bath Designer (CMKBD) and a Certified Interior Design (CID) in California. A CMKBD is a designer with substantial experience and training in both kitchen and bath design as it relates to construction, ergonomics, and safety. The "master" part of the designation is for designers who have held both the kitchen and bath designer certification for a minimum of 10 years.

I've been a professional kitchen designer for over 25 years and a sec-ond–generation designer as well. In the late 1970s, my father worked with my uncle running a custom cabinet shop. My mother started a kitchen design business at the same time. They were kitchen designers long before people even understood the term and when the first kitchen design course became available, they took it.

They operated a successful award–winning showroom for over 20 years in Canada, which was a large part of my life. I learned on the job and took every class on kitchen and bath design I could. In 1999, the economy forced us to close our showroom. My design mother and I were lured by the promise of sunshine and palm trees to Silicon Valley and eventually to an award–winning design/build firm in the East Bay just outside of San Francisco.

Over the years, I've designed kitchens for both new and existing homes, and in a variety of fascinating locations — beautiful log homes on the West Coast, a miniscule kitchen in a 200–year–old home blocks from the Bastille in Paris, an Australian kitchen near the Great Barrier Reef, as well as hundreds of kitchens of all types and descriptions in both Canada and the U.S. I've also been a judge for Canadian and U.S. national design competitions, as well as a 2–time judge for regional competitions.

In my spare time (between midnight and six), I write a blog on my website, *Kelly's Kitchen Sync*, where I discuss remodeling and design tips. In fact, that's where the idea for this book came from. If you've already visited my blog and recognize some of the tips, great and welcome! I hope you'll find many more to help you here.

The most important fact you'll ever learn about kitchen design

If you can take away anything from this book, paste these two sentences in big red letters somewhere you'll see them every day, and repeat them with every purchase you make:

Not all products work well in every kitchen.
Not all products are compatible with each other.

Almost every mistake, every "I–wish–I'd–known–before–I–bought" originates from those two facts. Whether it's flooring, a handle, or a ceiling light, every item has some quirk that eventually needs some attention to make your project run smoothly. Appliances change models every year, cabinetry lines vary, and some materials come and go.

> "…not all repairs or remodeling projects went smoothly
> for DIY respondents, with over one third (34%) having
> at least one regret stemming from trying to fix a broken
> appliance, installing tile, floors or cabinets…"
> **—Consumer Reports study of 1,000 Consumers.**
> [Used with permission by Consumer Reports]

If you're thinking, "Boy, this isn't something the home improvement shows ever mention", you're right. In this day and age of sunshine–y advertising, everything is perfect, isn't it? When a show only has 24 minutes plus commercials, time's short. No one wants to say, "Look, this is going to be a bit tricky. Let's be careful here."

Not that I'm here to be the Voice o' Doom. My clients have heard me chirp, "Kitchen design should be fun!" for years, and it is. If you understand the properties of all your kitchen products and how they interact with other products, you'll own the world (or at least your kitchen!)

Test Your Knowledge

Before we get started, let's get a sense of where you're at with the following questionnaire:

Read the question and circle the answer you think fits best

1. **What goodies are you planning for your new kitchen?**
   a) The basics. My counter is falling apart and I need to fix it now. I don't want to think about anything else for now.
   b) Some paint, a few knobs, maybe change light fixtures? Nothing huge.
   c) We're updating the cabinets, counters, appliances, floors, but not changing the walls…I don't think. I'm still figuring out the details.
   d) I want everything — and do I really need other rooms in the house?

2. **What grade of products are you planning to purchase?**
   a) Whatever I find at the local big store and/or the best deal.

b) Something decent that won't fall apart in the first 3 years.

c) Brand names I recognize.

d) As high-end and luxurious as I can get — integrated (built-in) appliances, custom counters and splashes. Not that I have an unlimited budget, but this is BIG!

3. **If you're planning on doing some of it yourself, what tools do you have?**

a) I have a hammer, I hammer in the morning, I hammer…wait. That's all I have.

b) A slick toolkit, a cordless drill and a couple other toys. I don't do too badly.

c) Some people call it the garage, but why keep cars, when you can have compound miter saws, air nailers, and enough tools to make *This Old House* crew weep.

d) The world is a safer place if I never touch a tool in my lifetime.

4. **How much of the design work do you want to be involved in?**

a) Not my interest. That's what other people are for.

b) I like looking at the magazines and I'm interested in knowing enough details to educate myself.

c) I'm fascinated about everything related to my kitchen. I know every TV show, participate in forums, and dream of the day my kitchen will be a reality.

d) I'm excited and involved, but my real goal is to be informed enough about all the terminology and processes to understand what my designer, contractor, and trade professionals are talking about.

5. **How much of the work are you planning to do yourself?**

a) Whatever's easy. Perhaps demolition, maybe painting. I've done that before.

b) I've done some work around the house, replacing light fixtures and I once tiled my vanity backsplash. It was okay.

c) I've got killer wood-working skills and the knowledge to install my own cabinets. Go me!

d) Ha ha ha! That's what professionals are for. I'm here to learn what they're doing and why.

How'd you do?

3 or more As: The Reluctant Remodeler

While it might have been something you planned, most likely something failed in your kitchen (dishwasher leaked, or the range died) and forced your hand. You don't want to do the work, but you need to know the best options, who to hire, even what questions to ask, so it can be fast, easy, and the value you need. Any help would be good.

3 or more Bs: The Cautious Planner

You've got some basic skills, and are willing to learn what you need, and maybe even a bit more. Will you DIY or not? You don't know yet, but you know enough that you want to research what's out there and avoid the most common mistakes.

3 or more Cs: The Enthusiastic DIY-er

You may not even be a DIY-er when it comes to the physical work, but you sure are when it comes to putting the design together. You're skilled enough to gut the kitchen (and stay away from structural changes.) You're keen to get going on the physical work, but you know that there's a bit more to the design and planning stages for a kitchen than almost anything else in the home.

3 or more Ds: The Informed Consumer

Unless you're a general contractor, or an architect, it's doubtful you'll tackle structural changes or additions on your own. However, even if someone else is tackling the work, you still want to make the selections and communicate with the crew in a reasonable manner. Like the Bs, you're an overseer — any insider tips which help smooth out the design phase will certainly pay off during construction.

Wait, I have a bit of everything!

Of course you do. You're my typical client. You may or may not have remodeled or built a kitchen before, hired folks successfully (or, ouch, not so successfully), and read a million books and websites. You know there's more out there.

So what does it mean?

Whether you're planning to remodel your kitchen on your own or someone else is helping you, it's a good idea to take stock of not only how much kitchen knowledge you have, but what your needs are. Can you change from an "A" to a "C" or any other combination during the planning stages? Absolutely. Can you learn to do the work yourself? Sure. There is no one–size–fits–all answer.

The questionnaire is meant to emphasize that different skill levels are a major contributing factor to your kitchen. It's also here to make you grin. Did it work?

How to make the book work for you

With that said, the book is divided into four sections:

The first section deals with expectations and reality — the unexpected emotional impact of home remodeling, and how the glossy photos and television design shows don't always show the incredible amount of work it takes to get the design right.

The second section deals with getting started — the nuts and bolts of the process — who does what, where to go, and which services might work best for you.

The third section is the largest: making your design work. I'll show you the common design mistakes on everything from cabinets to lighting and how to avoid them, along with some solid discussion into what makes good kitchen design work.

The fourth section deals with pulling it all together and a review of what to think of after your project is finished.

Commonsense Design

One of the challenges of growing up in the business and then writing this book is discovering that the terms I think everybody knows…they don't. I promise not to bombard you with terms — anything too technical will be explained as you read or mentioned in separate "Insider Definitions" sprinkled throughout the book.

If you're just starting out, don't worry if you feel a bit lost. Many of the ideas will begin to make sense as you become familiar with the process. If you're well into your research, hopefully this book will have you either nodding your head or rushing to check your design.

A pretty kitchen without proper function is not only useless, it's not very safe. I'd like to help you not only think like a designer, but give you some rock solid advice in a way that both easy and fun.

...Let's get started, shall we?

CHAPTER 2

LET'S START AT THE VERY BEGINNING

There was a time when kitchen design was easy, mainly because choices were so limited. There was a sink, a range, and a refrigerator (which was still optional in some parts of the continent). Cabinets were built in the home, and lighting consisted of one or two ceiling mounted lights. Mass manufacturing was the order of the day, and what one home had, so did the rest of the homes in the area.

At the beginning of my career, we complained about the lack of choices. Today we complain of having too many choices, so much so that it's almost a full-time job keeping up with new products on a daily basis, never mind yearly.

Now we deal with a minimum of 2–3 more appliances (dishwashers, microwaves, separate cook tops and wall ovens), multiple lighting choices (electrical, LED, hanging and recessed), international product selection, (tile and plumbing fixtures from Italy to New Zealand), different construction methods and climates, and far more. Kitchen design has become an extremely specialized field and even many professionals can run into trouble without experience or knowledge.

It's why my mantra from Chapter 1 bears repeating:

Not all products work well in every kitchen.
Not all products are compatible with each other.

The process

No wonder you feel confused and overwhelmed when you first start! Some of the longest faces I see are those in my showroom who announce, "I have to remodel my kitchen" with all the joy of facing a dental implant.

Even some of you who delight in choosing materials and products will feel some anxiety at least once, whether it's from interviewing the people who'll be installing your products or waiting for your refrigerator delivery. You don't know what to expect, and you're nervous that something might go wrong — which is perfectly natural. Do any of these sound familiar?

"I don't know where to start."
"There are so many horror stories out there."
"What if I select the wrong people?"
"What if I don't get what I like?"

As someone once asked me, "How do I know the question to ask when I don't know what the question *is*?" Good point.

There are also two hidden aspects, mainly confined to the remodeling, that may be at the root of your trepidation.

Firstly, *strangers* are coming into your home.

For the most part, our homes are our sanctuaries, our private domains, and our piece of the world cut away from the rest of the world. Some long–ago "fight–or–flight" hardwiring in our systems reacts negatively to this, whether you're aware of it or not.

The second reluctance deals with letting go of the old — cleaning out every nook and cranny, and getting rid of items that are no longer useful in our kitchens. As one of my clients once wistfully said, "You know I can't stand this kitchen, but there sure are a lot of good memories here. My children grew up in this kitchen. I didn't think I'd feel so wishy–washy about getting rid of it."

This can be challenging when you're faced with the old popsicle–maker that you haven't seen in years and you remember the delight on your

5-year-old's face (even if he's now 22, and doesn't eat sweets.) Or the fear that there is so much buried in the pantry or corner cabinet that it'll be impossible to get it clean in time. (Or we'll get stuck inside, and no one will ever find us again.)

Deep breath. It's all do-able.

Here are the stages many people go through:

Bewilderment

Sinks number into the hundreds, custom cabinet doors are almost infinite, and there are dozens of flooring choices to select first even before we choose color and style. Almost everybody contemplating a kitchen project starts here wondering what they're getting themselves into. Yes, it's a typical reaction and it will pass.

Asking friends for help

Many ask friends and family, "What do you like?" or ask the neighbor who just remodeled, "What did you pick?" In the beginning, the advice can sometimes both contradictory and confusing. "Cherry cabinets are in!" or "No, everyone is only picking painted cabinets." There can be a danger in asking for opinions too soon, which we'll talk about later.

Material selection

As you start to narrow your preferences, the information no longer seems as bewildering. You'll start noticing a common thread in your design searches. For example, as you pull photos from online and magazines, you might start noticing how most of the photos feature a farmhouse sink or most of the kitchens feature white cabinets. You might think you don't know what you like, but your mind does.

Working on the design

In some ways, this can be easier than other stages — what are you dreaming of for your future kitchen and what do you dislike about your present one?

Selecting your team

What do you want done in your kitchen, and who do you look for first? This depends on the scope of work and your talent (or lack of) for DIY. There are a lot more variations than simply designer, architect, and contractor. We'll explore some of the various options available so you can make the best choice for you.

Refining the design

Most consumers don't take this into account but it's an important factor in the design process. (Not all products are compatible with other... yes, you know.)

Finalizing

This includes ordering, signing contracts, cleaning out the cabinets. Of course, this isn't the final stage as your kitchen will now be under construction, but this is where I like to celebrate the "phew" moment, as in "Phew! We successfully waded through the maze and came out the victors on the other side!"

Everyone working in residential design and construction understands this process. We see it over the years with our clients and many of us have even gone through the process ourselves. Many of us are happiest when the work is over, like when the laundry or yard work is done, but unlike those two examples, the art of planning a kitchen can be a fascinating experience when you know what you're facing. It's the ultimate puzzle where the pieces are affected by our tastes and choices.

For those of you who have remodeled or built a new kitchen before, you may not realize how much things are changing, even over the past month, let alone the past few years. Advances in home technology have led to speed appliances and wireless products; there are new green building methods and green products all the time, and lifestyle changes in the family dynamics from adult sons, daughters, and grandparents moving under one roof have all created new options for how we design our kitchens.

As the dreaming starts...

...we should think practically. While a beautiful, functional kitchen is what we strive for, there are two key questions to ask:

1) **If it's a remodel, will it maintain or even increase the home value?**

   If you don't put enough quality into the home, it'll not only negatively affect the value (and therefore the resale value), but the quality might not last for the time you're living in the home.

2) **How long will you be living there?**

   I've always advocated on doing what you want, as long as you adhere to the minimum standards of the neighborhood. Here's why:

   No one can predict the trends, especially not now when everything is custom and styles are changing like clothes. Oh, we might predict one or two items, like the growing trend of induction, but we only have to study kitchens from the 1950s to today to see what I mean.

   There is no long term style when it comes to kitchen design, unless the design takes its inspiration from a set time period, such as a 200–year–old home. Even then, we're cheating with the new materials and products. In the past 60 years, refrigerators colors have changed from ballet pink to avocado green to stainless, with plenty of variation in between. And who in the 1980s could have predicted a bottom–mount freezer?

   So, who knows what people will want in their kitchens 10 or 20 years from now?

   Not only do trends change, but neighborhoods do as well. As an example, the older suburbs of San Jose, California are filled with 1950's-style homes. In the last decade, many of the original owners have moved or passed away. Formerly quiet retirement neighborhoods are giving way to lively young families. Where once the trend was for ordinary cupboards, tile counters, and basic single lighting, today's homeowners here want cabinet interior fittings, granite or quartz counters, and good lighting.

If you'd remodeled your home before the new group of younger homeowners and had replaced what was there, your home would suffer for resale. Could you have predicted it? Maybe, maybe not.

Of course there are exceptions, but if you're considering a major investment for your new kitchen, a chat with your local experienced real estate agent might prove beneficial.

"Eight in 10 (80%) consumers would like to change their kitchens (42% would 'change a few' things in their kitchens, 19% would 'change a lot,' and 19% would 'completely redo' their kitchens)." — **Kitchen and Bath Design News (from a consumer study report by RICKI, the Research Institute for Cooking and Kitchen Intelligence).**

Real estate perceived value

If you're thinking of short–term (2–5 years), keep an eye on the perceived value. Perceived value is what people believe determines quality and value of your home and it varies for every town, city, state, and country. For Boston, a formal dining room is an absolute; for San Francisco area, I'm designing some dining rooms as nooks and schoolwork offices.

Real estate agents refer to this as "comps" or comparative values to determine the market price. Don't install laminate and oak cabinets in a short term stay if other homes in your block have granite counters and maple cabinets. Your home won't command the same market value and might take longer to sell.

I've lived in 3 countries. Each area I've lived in has different design expectations than the one before, so I'm vastly entertained by any statements which start, "Oh, you must have…" or "Everybody has…" or my favorite, "That's the way it's done…" which is usually the exact opposite of the place I just moved from.

Perceived value is an uphill battle to fight, and one of the most challenging aspects to adjust. ("Vinyl flooring was good enough in the last place we lived. Why do I need tile?") No use fighting it, especially if you're not staying long — you need to match that comparative value.

I once watched a television show where a couple had completed a gorgeous contemporary kitchen — glossy cherry Italian slab doors, sleek gleaming European appliances, slate floors. It was to die for.

The problem was it was designed in a very traditional Southern city more suited to singing *My Dear Old Kentucky Home* than *Mambo Italiano*. The potential buyers wandered into the kitchen and froze. "Nice home, but the kitchen!" they said, in the same tones one might say, "Eww, a bug." It would have sold in a flash in San Francisco, or Seattle, or Calgary, but not there.

If you're in an area where there's a lot of non-locals moving in and out all the time — like San Francisco — then it's a little easier; eventually someone with the same ideas (or from the same place you came from) will come into town and weep with gratitude that you kept a breakfast nook (or something like that).

If you live in a town where they can count on one hand all the "new folks" who've moved into the area in the last century, you won't get far with breaking local traditions.

I still stand by my original thoughts — if this is your forever home, and then do what you want. If you're in an area where styles are traditional and you're planning a 10–20 year stay, I still say do what you want: the styles will change a lot within those next decades. We only have to look at the "new" homes of the 1980s to see how much.

Clients who have remodeled ahead of you offer their advice:
"I would have started packing earlier." — Here's your chance to get rid of the 3 containers of cinnamon hidden at the back of the cabinet, and that old coffee pot that hasn't worked in years. Fill one box a day as soon as you know, beginning with the items you don't use regularly. Avoid waiting until the last minute and working through the night.
"I would have done more research." — Kitchen materials can't just be pretty — they're work horses for your family and lifestyle. Two of the bigger misgivings in new kitchens are selecting the wrong products or the wrong quality.

Consider the period and style of your home

I jokingly label a kitchen that doesn't adhere to any of the architecture style and detailing of the home as a "Beetlejuice" kitchen, after the movie of the same name.

If you haven't seen the movie, the mother, an avant-garde artist, transforms the interiors of a traditional Victorian into hard contemporary. Think lots of grays, lack of moldings, and pointy metal sculptures. (The film is labeled a comedy but I jokingly call it horror.)

Even though this is a trend in Europe, where everything is old, it's not perceived as favorably in North America, especially in parts of the country where we can build modern homes. "The kitchen doesn't match the home!" is the phrasing you don't want to hear about your own home.

And yes, this can be a challenge for those of you who have a generic 1980s or 1990s home where there was no defining style.

While we can mix-and-match these days more than we ever could, try to avoid polar opposites, unless you or your team has at least a basic grounding in architectural history. For those of you who won't be hiring outside help, look at what's in the rest of the home — are there moldings? Are the ceilings low or high? What style are the windows and doors?

The emotional aspect of kitchen remodeling

If you ask why most people today want a new kitchen, they'll say "because it's old or outdated" or "the appliances don't work", or "I hate the color." But let's go deeper than that. What's the real reason?

You don't like it. It doesn't make you feel good.

Sure, the range is avocado-colored and no longer works—but you want to gut everything, and get a fresh start. Many of us place a lot of expectations on what that kitchen is supposed to do: "Now I'll plan some good parties" or "We can share proper family dinners" or "I can sit at my table and visit with my friends."

Did you notice that not one of those statements deals with the actual, physical function of the kitchen? No. They all deal with the emotional expectations, or what we hope the kitchens will achieve, not the actual food preparation.

Even for those of you saying, "Hey, I'd be happy if my burners worked", you'll still spend a lot of time looking for the range/cook top that satisfies your idea of what a "good" appliance should be.

Whether we recognize it or not, we're ultimately seeking spaces that make us happy to be in. We're hard-wired to react to color, light, and sound both positively and negatively.

Let's start here

There's a reason why you might hear, "Start your design process by finding pictures of kitchens you like."

While you worry you don't know what you want, your mind certainly does. Cut clippings from magazines you've purchased, or print out photos of kitchens you like. Stick them in a folder. Don't analyze any of them — just that you liked/loved/admired them as something you'd like.

I recommend sticky notes in different colors — say, blue for kitchens you love, and red for a detail, such as a backsplash. (It also helps if you write on the note what it is in the photo you like. I've had clients muttering as they show me the photos, "What did I like about that one anyway?")

Once you have a grouping, see if you can spot any common themes. Do you:
- *Select kitchens with light or dark counters?*
- *Select kitchens with lots of windows?*
- *Pick square rooms or curved?*

Sometimes you can't find a pattern. Or discover that you like both light and dark cabinets. Or you like everything, and nothing inspires you yet. That's okay. Some people need more steps in their processing to narrow their choices.

When it happens to my clients, we also try another trick — looking at what they *don't* like. Answers are sometimes faster and can be anything from colors ("I hate beige") or ("No white appliances") to (fill in the blank).

Also keep in mind many of the photos you see in magazines and books are fantasy kitchens — kitchens that even designers study to see what they can learn and apply. They aren't the reality of most North American kitchens. Many have the best architects and designers, the best craftspeople, the best real estate, and the best…well, you get the idea. Many, if not most of them, are priced well into 5–and 6–figures. If that's not in your budget, don't despair — there's something you can take away for your own use. Or search online — many homeowners are now posting photos of their finished kitchens on the internet.

Here are a couple of points to keep in mind:

- When you compare the kitchen photo you love, select photos where the ceilings are the same height as your kitchen. Custom hoods made of woods and metals look great in a ceiling that is 9 feet high, or higher, but look squat in kitchen with 8' ceilings. By keeping this one detail constant, it'll help you to visualize the space better.
- If you don't know why you like the kitchen photo, imagine removing all the decorations. Take away the dinner settings on the eating bar, the tray of muffins on the island, the plants, the pictures, the tables, and the chairs — do you still like the kitchen? Or was it the decorating you find you really liked? There's no wrong answer (and maybe points out the value of good décor).

Question your reasons

As a designer, I'm also looking for memories we've forgotten (which trigger either smiling recollections or knee–jerk reactions) as well as reactions to colors, textures, and shapes flavored by past experiences.

For example, I hate wallpaper with big, floppy flowers. I don't know why. It's coming back, and the colors are a lot better than the yellows, browns, and oranges I remember. Maybe it was something in my childhood: did I destroy some and get into trouble? Did it fall off my bedroom wall? Who knows? But I simply can't get enthused to this day about it. If you have that same type of emotional flinch, there's no use fighting it — it isn't something we can change easily.

Whatever you do, resist any and all attempts for someone to talk you into it. You're looking for things that make *you* feel good, not things that make others feel good.

On the other hand, it's amazing how much we cling to old reasons even when they're no longer valid. Questioning everything should be an important part of the process.

A client of mine badly wanted double ovens but the kitchen simply wasn't large enough. She resisted all attempts to select a space–saving range. Finally I asked, "Why double ovens?" She replied by opening the door on her old 27" wide oven, "Because a single oven isn't big enough for Thanksgiving. See?"

Ever had one of those light–bulb–over–your–head moments? Neither one of us had even discussed the oven width — I'd assumed she knew that new ovens were larger, and she was basing the design on what she knew. Once I pointed out that out (and we had a good laugh), we shopped for a 36" wide range with multi–level convection cooking. She fell in love and we were able to proceed.

What are your reasons?

---

3 Kitchen Myths: *We have a habit of copying the ways of our parents and grandparents "because that's the way it's been done"* — *even if the reason no longer applies. Here are the biggest leftovers from earlier ages.*

"Every kitchen needs a work triangle" — Out–dated for larger kitchens. Original source: the University of Illinois Small Homes Council–Building Research, 1946–1949. Note the date; also note the term small. There was a housing shortage after the Second World War and the race was on for affordable housing.

"Kitchen sinks must be centered under the window" — necessary when a kitchen had a 30" window and no electricity but not as necessary today in kitchens with 4–9 feet of kitchen windows.

Yes, I know it's a hot topic and, as always, it depends, but we'll talk about its history in greater detail in Chapter 11.

"Use semi-gloss paint in a kitchen" — Earlier generations dealt with moisture from canning and all day preparation of foods, smoke, and grease. Today's ventilation and better building eliminate the need for all but older homes.

Dig past the surface

Along with promotional consideration, we have a slew of advertising, especially where there are channels devoted to all things related to maintaining and altering our homes. The shows are filled with the best, often the most expensive, and often way beyond most people's budgets, with the unspoken message, "Nothing but the best will do."

Poppycock.

Manufacturers have a vested interest in creating a demand for their product. While it's nice to want something, half of the challenge is discovering what you really need vs. what you're being told you need.

One doesn't have to trump the other—by all means, if you really want something, and it fits within your lifestyle, have it. But a top–of–the–line professional range won't turn you into Martha Stewart if you're not a serious cook–it takes work and a steep learning curve, especially for beginners. If you're prepared for it and think it might be fun; that's a different story. A lot of my clients went from not very interested in cooking to surprising themselves with how much they enjoyed experimenting in their new kitchens.

Allow time to discover the physical properties of your wish list and how well the products will withstand your family's lifestyle.

Did you know a professional range won't make your life faster and easier? Sure, it'll cook your food faster because it's hotter than regular ranges — but a pro range is messy. High heat means splatter, and spills instantly burning on the surface, and more cleaning and scrubbing than you might be currently used to. In a restaurant, the chef doesn't clean the range. He or she has kitchen help which, unfortunately, isn't part of your appliance package.

Not that I'm picking on the professional ranges — it's simply that they take more work to clean than a regular range and if you don't know that going in, you might be unpleasantly surprised. Take some time to discover the physical properties of your wish list and how well the items will stand up to your family's lifestyle.

Listen to that inner voice

"I wish I had…" is one of the most painful sentences in kitchen design. My function as a designer is to pay attention to what you're saying about your likes and lifestyle, and point out pros and cons of each choice, even if sometimes you don't want to hear it, so that you can make an informed decision.

There are so many choices available that I might suggest some flexibility built in to your decision process. I once had a client who wanted a fireclay sink but for budget reasons reluctantly decided on stainless. Every time we met, she brought up the fireclay sink — how beautiful it was, and how she'd seen someone else's, etc. After the sixth or seventh time, we (my designer mother and I) suggested that while the sink was indeed over the budget, our client would have truly regretted her stainless choice long after the kitchen was finished and the budget was forgotten, and we told her so. Once she realized how many times she brought it up, she agreed, and chose the fireclay sink. As soon as the kitchen was done, she was thrilled. She's never regretted it for a second.

Don't ignore your inner voice. You know better than you think you do. If you don't have a designer, here's a suggestion. As you go through the process, ask your friends to keep an ear out for items you continuously circle back to, and repeat your words back to you.

Can't decide? Throughout the process, imagine your kitchen finished both with the item and without it. Think about how

much you spent for it, and how much use you'll get out of it.
If you have a niggling doubt, best to confront it before you
order or the construction starts.

What if you don't have an inner voice?

If you're a Reluctant Remodeler or the type that simply can't get excited about the idea of a new kitchen and everything looks fine, then in some ways, your selection process is easier. You don't care that the cabinets come in four thousand finishes — just give you something easy-to-clean and the same color as the rest of your furniture.

You still have some of the same homework. Consider:

- The products' properties as well as the longevity and durability that relates to the family lifestyle.
- Checking reviews, whether they're consumer-or editorial-based, can also be a sound approach.
- Finding the right retail people with both experience and professionalism.

Don't let others tell you what you should have

Out of all the rooms in the home, the planning of kitchens is eerily similar to a family wedding. Everyone — from family, friends, co-workers, and even the cashier at your local grocery store — has an opinion.

The fact is, many family and friends live vicariously through your new kitchen to the point that their "advice" is more what *they* wish for than what is actually beneficial for you and your lifestyle — much like the family offering advice on the dress of the new bride, regardless of her opinions. They mean well, but in a lot of cases, they're really projecting their wishes and dreams on you.

Over the years, clients have shared stories of strangers who've knocked on the door expecting a tour, friends determined to enforce all their decisions regardless of what my client wants, aunts who love a particular color that they insist should be added without regard of the homeowner's preferences. Only recently, I observed a potential client who waited until her interior decorator friend (who hadn't been hired but took over the entire meeting) left the store to confide that she disliked what her friend was suggesting but didn't know how to tell her 'no'.

Have I seen some excellent suggestions from friends and family that made perfect sense for the kitchen owner? Of course.

My advice? Remain non-committal until you have a better sense of what you'd like. Tell your friends, neighbors, co-workers that you'll "take it under advisement". If you have a design professional helping you, let him or her act as your buffer.

If it's your design professional that isn't giving you good reasons for their advice, and you're feeling pushed, time to start addressing those concerns, or look for another professional.

It's all about doing your homework, and discovering that perfect balance of what best suits you emotionally and physically.

PART 2
GETTING STARTED: COSTS, WHERE TO GO, AND WHO YOU NEED

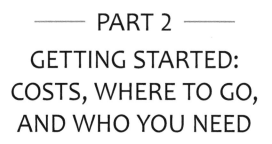

CHAPTER 3

HOW MUCH WILL IT COST?

I wish I could reach through the pages and pronounce a number for every one of you.

Sorry.

There is very little that is the "same" in this field any longer, from product selection to our own taste levels. (Don't believe me? Enter any professional or consumer forum and ask for an opinion. Some might even match.)

In this chapter, I want to help you avoid the "here's what I expected it to cost and here's what it actually does, oh help" stage.

Knowing where your costs add up is half the battle

It doesn't mean that you have to start with a kitchen stripped of all the goodies that you really want, but a basic kitchen has fixed items — from code requirements to permits to your basic design and labor charges.

It should include what you feel is non-negotiable — the extra glazing on the cabinets, a counter-depth refrigerator, a custom green counter vs. solid surfacing, or a fully loaded kitchen.

For example, you might have a gorgeous ceiling light priced in your head, but you might not have accounted for:

- Who picks up the light? (If shipped, is anyone home to receive deliveries? Many home deliveries are "drop-shipped" to save money, which means it's parked either to the curb or the garage. A chandelier isn't so bad; a tall pantry with rollout shelves can be a challenge.)

- Who assembles it? Some lights ship in many separate pieces.
- Who repairs both the sheetrock/coffered ceiling/texture?
- How it will be switched? Will the wall be opened up and the drywall need to be removed, or is it possible for the electrician to partially thread to save the walls?
- Who textures the walls and ceiling, and paints it?

Very few people think of all the steps involved in not only design, but assembly and installation. And when we're dealing with a kitchen, there are not only a lot of pieces, but each one requires various levels of skill on the part of your team.

As we move along ever more into custom design, you'll hopefully begin to comprehend why getting a "quote" on the kitchen without detailing the specifics in advance is a bit of a lost cause.

What you should know about dream kitchens

You're watching your favorite design program. The voice-over says, "This kitchen was only $20,000.00 with granite, custom cabinets, mosaic-inlaid floors, pro appliances, and handmade backsplash tile." You take careful notes, and go shopping — only to fall over in shock. Why is your kitchen — which is much smaller than the ones on television, by the way — $50,000.00?

Before you accuse your local business of taking advantage, welcome to the wonderful part of television called "promotional consideration." Many of the products for shows are provided for free in return for being on the show. In other words, if the producers had to pay for everything they're showing you, the price most likely would have been $50,000.00.

It's a bartering system: "We'll supply our cabinets for your show, Ms. Producer, and in return, you mention them at least 2 times, and show our logo at the end of the show."

In some ways, it makes sense. Given the cost of products, no production company could afford to finance an entire season of kitchens. Manufacturers know their place on a popular show will guarantee them some strong sales. It's a win–win for both.

However, it's an unspoken part of the business — and it doesn't do any of us any favors out in reality land. That's why you're confused and upset. It's also why designers, builders, and architects get that pained look on their faces when anyone mentions design shows.

Is a good deal really that good?

In this field, if it sounds too good to be true…it probably is. Yes, sometimes there really are going–out–of–business deals, and wonderful stories on how someone got a deal on custom tile that was never picked up, or an entire set of high–end cabinets at a local re–use store. They aren't the norm.

Sorry to be the spoilsport, but I've really seen so much that I know I'm overcautious — I've seen products come and go, come and fail, and for the past few years, a great deal of misinformation about quality.

When someone tells you, "You can get the same dovetail drawer box and the same hardware as Fancy X Brand for half the price"? I've rarely found it to be true. Logical reasons for price differences usually point out to a company going out of business, selling an imitation, or — your luck — using the product as a lost leader. (A lost leader is a product in a store that is sold below cost to draw you into the store in the hopes you'll buy other products. It "leads" the advertising page, but any profit is "lost.")

Rarely are there super deals in the mid–to–high end. The only way to make a product less expensive is to cut corners either with the quality or the labor. Both are possible with outsourcing, but imitations neither last as long or carry much in the way of a warranty.

Can there be good deals in a lesser quality? Of course there can, but there are no super deals for like quality unless as outlined above. It's like saying there is no difference between couture and knock–offs — even the quality of thread is different.

On the other hand, there may be some factors that are simply not important to you. That's fine. If you don't notice difference between the various photographic grades of vinyl flooring, and the quality and durability are similar, is there really a need to spend the extra money? Not if it isn't important to you and all other factors are equal.

Insider Definition: *Trades, or trades people, or trade professional*—defines the people who specialize in a "trade" or particular installation process in your home, such as plumbers, installers, framers, and electricians.

Getting the "Wow" factor without blowing the budget

My mother is fond of relating how French women dressed in the '50s and '60s and comparing it with design. "They'd wear a basic black dress, not too expensive, but spent money on the accessories — a drop–dead scarf, the purse, and/or the shoes. They made the entire outfit look expensive without breaking the bank."

Translated: keep the big–ticket items neutral and cost–effective, and spend the money on quality accessories.

Consider these ideas:

- Change out the cabinet handles and knobs: really good architectural handles may be expensive, but a few in a key viewing spot will add a bit of sparkle. For an existing kitchen, make sure the handles will fit the existing handle screw holes.
- Install laminate or wood counters: there are some amazing colors in laminate counters these days. Wood counters, while not the most durable of products, are also inexpensive.
- If you can't afford to install granite on your entire counter (and you won't be replacing your cabinets for a very long time), install a section on your island only.
- Buy and install decorative new lighting.
- Paint the cabinets or walls. First thing my real estate agent suggested

to me when I sold my home was: "Let's freshen up the rooms with a coat of paint." Freshen up is a good term.

- Add some decorative trim — corbels or crown mold—to your existing cabinets.

- Change your baseboards. Be careful with this one — it can get pricey and frustrating to do yourself if you're in an older home or one where the floor isn't even.

- Keep your trim the neutral paint color, or the same wood stain, throughout the home. It'll not only maintain a consistency throughout the home, it'll save on extra cans of paint that are only partially used.

A final tip

There are two ways of assembling your early budget. Select everything you want so you can price and save accordingly, or start with the basic layout and design, and add the options according to their importance.

Either way, I'd like to provide you with a guideline of items most people forget to add. These are *in addition to the materials and products* and most are simply the costs associated with installing the products.

What parts of the design are more expensive than others?

If your house is built on a concrete slab floor and your budget is tight, it can be costly to break up that slab to install plumbing on an island. (And for the slab floors called post–tension that have bars installed in the slab, it's to be avoided at all costs.) Removing a load–bearing wall is costly in terms of re–building the framing and footings to carry the load, and you still have to add the cost of engineering. Removing a window in a 100–year–old home which has a custom wood siding which is not made any longer will be an additional factor to your design budget. Don't be afraid to weigh the cost vs. value early on.

What construction details might add to the cost?

Those of you planning new homes have an easier time because you're starting fresh. For those of you with older homes, is there enough insulation in the walls, floors, and ceilings? Is there water damage at the sink? Are you planning on relocating doors or windows or removing a wall? If so, might there be plumbing hidden inside or will you need to relocate outlets and switches?

Will the electrical panel or wiring need upgrading?

Many of the new appliances have higher electrical needs today. Will the panel carry the load of the new appliances and lighting? Is the wiring and electrical up to code? Will you only replace the covers on the kitchen side, or replace all the colors so they match in the entire kitchen/nook and on all the walls?

What prep work will the flooring require?

Not all floors can be easily removed or replaced without hard work scraping or sanding or simply tearing up. What is the existing flooring and how much prep work will the new floor require? Will they require new baseboards or door casings and will they need to be painted or stained?

What is the existing condition of the plumbing?

In older homes — especially in older homes — we can expect some water damage or leaky pipes. Is the existing plumbing leak–free, or are there old cast–iron pipes which require replacing? Is the drain installed in the wall or buried at the back of the cabinet?

How easy are the appliances to install?

Some are easy enough to install yourself, while others require a licensed, factory trained installer to maintain the warranty. Some take less than an hour to install, while others take half a day. What electrical and plumbing will need to be modified for the actual installation?

Replacing doors and windows isn't always simple.

The thickness of your walls and the materials that cover the interior and exterior walls affect the installation. What casings and trims will be used and who will stain and paint them?

Where is your current HVAC — heating and ventilation?

Are there any radiators or forced air vents that need relocation and/or repair?

What is your wall and ceiling texture?

Sometimes, we can't simply repair one wall; the entire ceiling and rest of the room need to be textured. Here, I have 8 different styles of texturing from rough to smooth and they all vary in cost and the amount of time they take to complete.

What is your final painting choice?

Lighter colors cost less than dark colors because they take less coats of paint to apply on the wall. Will the painting cover just the walls — or the walls, doors, trim, and ceiling? Is there wallpaper to be removed? Or paint on doors to be sanded off?

Now is your chance to avoid surprises. That's what proper design planning is all about. Check your local building codes and regional building codes. There's no use tearing up your kitchen only to discover the electrical panel needs upgrading before your new appliances will work. Knowing what to expect saves both emotional stress and the length of time to complete a project.

CHAPTER 4

DIY — WHERE ARE THE SAVINGS?

How much will I really save if I do it myself?

You know this is a very brave chapter to write, don't you? No matter what I mention, someone out there is going to tell me there's another way. Or tell me it can't be done that way where you live.

DIY, or do-it-yourself, is as varied as kitchens. I know for many of you, DIY is a joy and a curiosity and a great feeling of pride to see the fruits of your own creativity and hard work. Everyone has different skill levels, and every area has its own expectations, building methods, and climates.

If you're not a DIY-er, skip forward to the next chapter…unless you're acting as your own general contractor which we'll cover in this chapter.

Most of the questions I receive in the showroom and on my blog are on how to save money. For those of you who are venturing into your first project, I hope I can provide some insight so that it'll be a success and you can bask in that "I-did-it" afterglow.

I also think that some DIY reality shows have a lot to answer for. They make it look so easy (just tear down this non-structural wall and open up the kitchen to the dining room), while omitting vital details (did you turn off the electricity bef–zap!)

There's a fine line between "it's so easy even a baby can do it!" and "don't attempt this at home without 3 paramedics and a pint of ice cream on stand-by." DIY forums sometimes oversimplify, and we professionals, who have seen (and rescued) many homeowner projects and know everything that can go wrong, might sound a bit Chicken Little to you. (The sky is falling, the sky is falling!)

Most answers, of course, are somewhere in–between.

If you've never done any do–it–yourself work before, you're already facing a steep learning curve.

And yes, experience does make a difference, but there are levels of experience needed that we'll walk through together.

Projects such as tearing out the flooring (unless there's asbestos in the floor), or removing wallpaper (there are many tricks to make it easier), are simple enough and can save you money.

However, the installation of a product often shows the skill level of the installer. I've been to homes where the cabinet doors don't hang quite right, or there are bulges in the flooring. I've also seen woodworking so fine I wheedled the homeowner to come and work with us. (It never worked, darn it!)

It's a challenge to estimate costs around the continent due to costs of living and regional preferences (and I'm sure to get flack from some if they don't fall within my ranges) but I'll attempt to list my thoughts on prices at various points throughout this chapter, so at least it might give you a basis.

Before we do that, let's break this down by skill levels, starting with the most advanced to the easiest:

#1. Experienced DIY: *Acting as your own general contractor*
#2. Advanced DIY: *Projects that take a bit more skill*
#3. Basic DIY: *Sweat equity and enthusiasm*

We'll start with the experienced as there are some important tips that even for Reluctant Remodelers should consider:

#1. Experienced DIY: *So you want to be your own general contractor*

I could have also added "Experienced...or super organized." Homeowners have acted as their own general contractor for years. In many cases, you're not hindered by the safety rules and regulations that govern our industry, but that can also lead to some dangerous mistakes. If the following seems a bit excessive to those of you who've successfully self-contracted with no worries, please keep in mind I've heard some truly horrific stories over the years, so I'm going to err on the side of caution. No one should have to say, "Nobody told me about that!"

If you haven't done any remodeling before, and you decide that you'll act as general contractor yourself, here are some of the details you'll need to know.

Are you a good scheduler?

There is quite a bit of work juggling 3 or more trades, and knowing the timelines for all. If you're planning on acting as a homeowner/general contractor for the first time, understand that you will run into scheduling and material delays, not because you're a homeowner, but because it's the nature of the business.

It takes some skill to not only schedule the trade professionals, also known as sub-contractors or colloquially as subs — the plumber, tile setter, or cabinet installer, to name a few. You might face that the inspector wants a correction before you move forward, or weather might delay the arrival of your windows or cabinets — any and all of these scenarios are possible (I discuss them further on).

In fact, expect a scheduling delay to happen at least once during your project, *no matter how organized you are.*

Think of it like an airplane rolling down the runway, scheduled to take off at a certain time. If it's late, it has to be re-shuffled back into the line-up, often causing delays to every single plane behind it. If every plane misses, then the entire system becomes snarled.

A change in your schedule means a reshuffling of any where from 3–10 jobs for a sub-contractor in a week. Most times, the sub-contractors are used to it — unless their client (you) constantly reshuffles every single day. Do it too many times, and your job will have to be fit between others, simply because you missed your window of opportunity. And if you keep changing the schedule enough, your project will drop down the priority list.

What you don't want to do is schedule all the work at once in the same area. This is a beginner mistake and one that can cause more delays rather than less. If your workers are constantly tripping over each other, there's a possibility of damage.

The worst project I ever saw was a new home build, with all the subs working at once in the kitchen. All of them were mad because they couldn't get finished and had to wait for others. There were electrical shavings all over the freshly finished floor, which had been trampled on by the installers and the plumbers before the electrician could sweep up. The floor refinisher blamed the electrician, and the electrician blamed the counter person for sweeping the shavings onto the floor. The counter people blamed the electrician for scratching the counters.

This is not the norm, thank goodness. In this type of scenario, no one wins — it takes extra time for the trades to do their work, there's too great of a possibility of damage, and no one will take responsibility. Schedule your sub-contractors one after the other and let them perform what they do best.

Can you get the materials to the jobsite on time?

Half the work is making sure you're not holding anyone up by not having the products delivered on time. Will the lumber come when you need it? Will you have the plumbing supplies delivered? Do you have your material supplier on speed dial?

Okay, I'm joking about the last part, but there is nothing worse than finding out that you've arranged the framer for the first of the month and discovering the windows aren't coming until the end.

This is why I don't joke about contracting: it's a tough job and you'll be on the phone or with your plans from 6am–10pm at night, making calls, arranging deliveries, and overseeing the project to make sure that the drawings were correct, and the project runs smoothly.

Do you know your local city, state/province and country building codes?

They're not as important if you're doing cosmetic work such as changing those cabinet handles or painting, but you need to know what the codes are for any building work, electrical, or plumbing.

If you're planning on acting as your own general contractor, you should know, or have access to, a code book. Code is the minimum building safety standards allowable. Most of the US and Canada adhere to the International Building Codes (found at http://www.iccsafe.org). In addition, there are also state and local business codes, National LP (liquid propane)–gas codes, electrical codes, mechanical codes, concrete and masonry codes, and some states have individual energy codes.

Taunton Press publishes condensed code check guides on building, plumbing, mechanical and electrical codes that I use for quick reference. You can find them at:
http://www.codecheck.com/cc/ccwwwbuy.html

Do you have a good knowledge of construction?

If you know nothing about buildings or structure, or about the amount of weight your home will bear, and you're planning a major remodel, hire a general contractor.

I once drove out to home of a client whose husband was acting as GC (general contractor). It was a two–story home, and they were planning on removing a wall between the kitchen and family room to make room for a larger kitchen.

Apparently, it was taking too long, as far as the wife was concerned, so when her husband was at work, she took a sledge hammer to the wall, and took it out herself. We were standing in the empty shell of a kitchen.

"Hubby had been lagging getting this done," she said proudly. "So once he saw I'd taken some action, he couldn't move fast enough."

Of course he couldn't. She'd removed the bearing wall of the home — the roof was sagging badly. The husband had two 4×4 posts up, more as a toothpick prop than anything else.

"I bet," I said. I never did hear from them again but I wonder if he ever relayed to her that she'd almost caved their roof in.

All I'm trying to say is: consider personal and family safely, especially when planning a remodel with all your family still living in the home.

Employer responsibility and permits

Permits are acquired from your local city or county building department before you start work. The city has inspectors who perform safety checks to determine the project is being built to local safety codes. You may not need them if you're doing non–structural work and/or not relocating electrical or plumbing (but it's different for every part of the continent, so best to check with your local building department before you start.)

As soon as you hire sub–trades, then you're considered an employer, and should be carrying Worker's Compensation. Check to see if your home insurance will cover any accidents during the construction.

In California, for example, you are personally liable for any injuries and deaths at your home. Check your own state or province regulations.

Mechanic's Liens: Trades working in your home have the right to protect themselves in case of non–payment by recording mechanic's lien against your home. Depending on your location, non–payment might force foreclosure or make your home impossible to sell until you pay off the lien. In the case of most liens, there is additional paperwork afterwards that must be signed off by the tradesperson to indicate you've paid them in full.

This is one of the reasons for the higher costs of a professional, licensed and bonded contractor — they're responsible for the integrity of the work they perform. What does your state or province require?

Four remodeling points everyone should know

One of the misconceptions that I find odd about this business is the expectation everything in a remodel should run smoothly. In all the years I've been in design, I can count on both hands the number of times that's happened. There's always something that tests everyone's mettle: a handle that's scratched, a tile order that is out of stock (which seems to happen after ensuring multiple times that the tile was in stock).

As a designer once stated, "We are the buffer between client and the product until it's installed." The "we" includes the contractor, the architect, the designer and everyone else in the trade. Now, with the advent of online shopping, and DIY design, the rest of you get to see the challenges we face on a regular basis. *These are the biggest four:*

1) **Delivery damage**

   A great many things can happen between the manufacturer/store/ company to your home (and usually do). Take loading cabinets, for example. There's a special way to load the tall cabinets first, to lay the fronts face–to–face, to place cardboard or blankets in certain areas, etc. — all to avoid the cabinets (or appliances or counters) shifting in transit. Snow, an accident on the road, or a swerve to avoid another driver — any one of these can show up as a dinged corner, or a broken drawer face, or a destroyed box.

   It's why we employ talented installers and contractors — they have the skill to repair a lot of delivery mistakes. It's been part of professional remodeling as long as I can remember.

   But many beginners simply don't realize this, and it accounts for a massive amount of wasted indignation on forums from all but the experienced DIY-ers. They have the same air of resigned expectation we do.

   The push for cheaper and cheaper transport has also pushed a large number of professional truckers out of business. I don't see this improving in the near future, no matter how much we all wish for perfection.

2) **Not ordering enough materials**

   Did you order exactly what you need? Don't. Order *more*. If you order tile, expect tile chips or a broken piece or two. Unlike retail, unless you're paying top dollar (and even then), you're going to find some flaws with a product.

   As an example, our design/build firm prefers to order the materials because we keep a handle on delivery timelines as well as understand the quirks of each product. A client thought he would save money by ordering his wood flooring elsewhere. He came to me later, saying: "I found almost two boxes of short cuts, and blemished wood pieces." He was outraged. I was so startled, I blurted, "You were lucky." Even with the most expensive line of wood, I can still expect some flawed boards.

Allow 10%–20% overage for custom or special order tile, so if you need 100 square feet of tile, order 110–120 feet. Flooring can be about 10%, more if it's a special diagonal lay or border. I've moved away from ordering any Italian tile after too many promises of "It's in customs and will be delivered any day now!" For months.

Eventually the tile showed up, but it kept the kitchen in construction limbo for longer than it took to complete the entire project had tile arrived on time.

Expect to order extra trim, such as scribe molding, for cabinet repair. It might seem like an unnecessary expense when you buy it at the beginning, but it'll be a real time–saver if it is needed. Your installer won't have to wait for 2–4 weeks for a new piece to arrive, and you won't be in danger of trying to book your installer to come back and install it after he's already onto his next project. (Apologies to those builders who scribe panels on–site and/or build your own cabinets. A bit harder to do here in earthquake country.)

3) **Out–of–stock/delays**

This doesn't happen on a regular basis, but it does happen. "Yes, it's in stock. We have 3,000 feet in Sacramento/Duluth" usually means it's available the week you called with no guarantees it'll be in any time after that — especially in a growing economy where everyone is ordering the same item. It doesn't take long for the 3,000 feet of material to sell out.

There is almost always a delay on some segment of appliances — a microwave trim piece, or a vent cover for a chimney–style fan.

I take the stance that I'd rather have the item earlier and know I have it and it's ready to go than make the trades wait around for its arrival.

4) **Time of year**

Seasonal changes often play havoc with the schedule. For example, spring floods can affect anything shipped by boat or barge. Summer time is when everyone is building, and ordering, so timelines for ordering may be longer. Fall windstorms can shut down your power, or knock down trees. Winter blizzards often delay anything shipped cross–country by truck and freight train. As long as you're aware of the possibilities, you can mentally prepare yourself and adjust your schedule accordingly.

#2. Saving money for Enthusiastic DIY–ers

I know a few enthusiastic DIY–ers. Some are even so skilled they could set up shop. Their favorite fascination is their home and how to make it better using their own talent and sweat equity. *For those of you with years of wood-working and carpentry skills, you might tackle the following projects:*

Cabinet installation

Cabinets aren't as easy to install as most people think. For very simple projects — a galley kitchen or a small L–shape with an island — cabinet installation is do–able, especially with a stock or semi–custom cabinet, but I'd definitely classify most kitchen layouts as intermediate and advanced DIY. Cabinets have to be set square even if the walls and floor aren't (if they aren't, you'll never be able to adjust the doors and drawers). I've seen a lot of first–timers run into difficulty with installing an entire kitchen. If you don't know how to deal with square cabinets and crooked walls and/or don't have the compression nail–guns, or table — and compound–miter saws for the job, strongly consider hiring an installer.

Tip: 20%–50% of the cabinetry is a rough rule of thumb for the installation costs you might save — the more complex, the higher the price. The easiest kitchens are the ones with no corners — walls don't form a perfect 90-degree corner, and fitting the cabinets and counters can sometimes be a challenge even for the experienced. Installation can be priced in a couple of ways — per piece or as a complete job.

Wood or laminate installation

Wood butcher block and pre–formed laminate (that's the counter with the rolled front edges) are relatively inexpensive and easy to install compared to stone, tile, or quartz. The wood can be cut on–site by anyone while the laminates can be cut to fit by a counter top shop for minimal cost.

Tip: Surprisingly, you're not saving a lot on installation; the main reason people select these tops is a) the materials themselves are much cheaper than stone, and b) they're relatively easy to install (again, providing the corners of the kitchen are a perfect 90-degrees and the walls aren't wavy.) If money is the priority here, focus on how much money you're saving on material choice instead.

Complex tile backsplash

Adding borders, inlays and other details might not worry you, but you should do some drawings first to make sure that your details are worked out before starting. You don't want the electrical outlets or switch plates, for example, covering your decorative tile or liner, and you may need to calculate if the outlets will need to be raised or lowered.

Tip: Complex tile installations vary from $ 600–$1800 for particularly ornate splashes in a 12×14 u-shaped kitchen, depending on backsplash heights, the type of tiles, and how ornate the splash is.

Flooring

Installing anything from vinyl to stain–in–place wood won't be too much of a challenge for your experience, and again, less expensive (and complex) if the room is square and there aren't a lot of doors or radiators, or room transitions. Some of the flooring options, such as click–lock or snap in place laminate flooring are more DIY–friendly than say, installing and refinishing a ¾" solid wood floor (although some of you out there could definitely handle it).

Potential trouble–spots

Electrical and Plumbing

For those of you who know where the plumbing shut-off valves are, or for those of you who can identify a shut–off valve in the first place, removing and installing a new sink and/or hooking up a dishwasher might not be a challenge. Same goes for those of you who understand rudimentary electricity — it's not difficult to re-wire a new ceiling fixture.

Proceed with caution

Anything that can explode, start a fire, or flood your home—gas, electrical, and water—isn't a standard DIY project. If you don't know that you should turn off the circuit breaker before you change that lighting fixture, or shut off your water supply before switching out the sink, let a licensed professional handle it.

Gas for cook top and ranges

Do you know how to calculate the gas pressure and pipe size required for your new cook top? If there are already too many appliances (gas dryer, water heater, multiple fireplaces) running off your home's main gas supply line, there won't be enough pressure for the new cook top and the flame will never be be high enough. Gas is like water. Not enough pressure and your gas appliances will sputter.

The same applies for electricity, especially when it comes to adding new appliances. One of the biggest fire hazards in a home is overloading anything electrical—whether it's using a 150w bulb in a 75w socket, or adding a 48" professional range to a 100 amp electrical panel which is already drawing 120 amps on the line. A home from the 1960s or earlier never planned for dishwashers, double ovens, air conditioners, hot tubs, bar refrigerators, and/or indoor/outdoor kitchens that we have today.

As an electrician once told me, the reason for each and every electrical code came from someone dying. If you're adding extra appliances or lighting but don't know how to calculate electrical load, hire an electrician.

Stone counter installation

Avoid self–installation of stainless steel, and both real and manufactured stone counter tops. I'm starting to see "order your own granite" online, which I think is a dangerous idea. Stone is heavy, and most people don't have the cranes and winches to move the slabs. There have been incidences of people being crushed to death from being at the wrong place when slabs were being moved in stone yards. Now imagine what could happen when you and your friends are lifting half-a-ton of stone that's been drop-shipped to the garage and you have to get it up the stairs to the kitchen.

Windows and doors

There isn't a cross-continent standard. Not only does every period and style of house have different requirements, but so do the regions the home is located in, the window brands, and whether the home is new or remodeled. I'm not convinced there is much cost savings to remodel your windows if you've never done it before, and a lot of potential for leaking.

Tip: You have a better chance with interior doors, especially if you're changing out the frame as well (retro-fitting a door into an existing (and possibly crooked) frame takes some skill most beginners don't have. Labor costs may depend on the experience, speed, and knowledge of the installer.

A final note

Don't forget to check your local codes and read your specifications until you can mutter them in your sleep. There's no use installing a great kitchen and finding out that you should have left 18" of clearance between the gas range burners and the underside of your very flammable wall cabinets.

#3. Saving money if you're a Reluctant Remodeler or a Cautious Planner:

Demolition

It's not difficult to demolish a kitchen, but you should proceed with caution.

Find out how your location city/town wants you to dispose of the materials. In my area, for example, we're required to separate the demolished materials into recycled (old appliances or lumber) and non-recycled (drywall and broken lamps). The appliances are further separated for delivery to our local metal yard. That's three separate trips, and possibly four, if anything can be donated to Habitat for Humanity or Goodwill or the local re–use and recycle in your town: www.freecycle.org

---

You'll save anywhere from 16 hours of labor (2 people, 1 day) to 32 hours depending on the size. Don't forget to factor in the cost of a truck, travel time, and trash costs. Some states and provinces have stringent recycle programs in effect, which may result in several trips to various recycle and re–use places.

Insulation, sheetrock, and taping

Only exterior walls have insulation, unless you want some soundproof-ing between interior walls. (Standard insulation in interior walls only provides minimal noise reduction. A soundproofing drywall/sheetrock like QuietRock is much better.) The 4'×8' panels of sheetrock were a bit tough to lift all by someone like me (I can do it but it's not easy) and taping and sanding is a time–consuming, dusty, and thankless job. I didn't do it properly the first time and was sanding for days. You're not really saving that much, and you'll spend four times the amount of time an experienced tradesperson will.

Insulation and sheetrock isn't that expensive. Find the correct R–values for your insulation in your area. U.S. Energy Star Website
(www.energystar.gov)
Canada's Mortgage and Housing Corporation
(www.cmhc–schl.gc.ca)

Backsplash tile

Simple tile patterns in ceramics, limestones, marbles, and porcelain tiles aren't too difficult, especially if you have a good tile saw. Unless you're truly an expert, avoid installing glass and metal tiles; they take a special skill level that even most well-experienced DIY-ers might hesitate.

DIY backsplash installation has a potential labor savings of anywhere from $400.00 for a simple backsplash to $1,000.00 for a complex, 15 feet by 1½ foot high full backsplash on three walls. Don't skimp over researching the proper way to prepare grout—there are professional forums which discuss nothing but the mixing, preparation, and tile factors that affect grout.

Installing cabinet handles

If you've got a drill and a level, cabinet handles and knobs are not that difficult to install. Making a template that can fit over each door and drawer can save a lot of time and aggravation.

Tip: $1.00–$5.00 per handle, depending on complexity. Not much of a savings unless you have 40 or more handles. Special care should be taken with recessed drawer panels, as the screw length needs to be longer.

Painting

Painting is like sewing. It's the preparation that takes all the time — the caulking of doorways, the sanding, the cleaning of particles off the wall, and the taping off areas you're not planning to paint — and not the actual painting. In the scale of preparation and skill, painting walls are much easier than cabinets or doors and windows. If you don't take the time to prepare, your painted finishes will reflect it.

Painting prices varies so much, I can't even begin to offer a price, but I can offer this: never buy cheap rollers, brushes, or paint. If the work isn't standard—high ceilings or painting the cabinets, for example, you'll definitely save time and aggravation by hiring a pro.

Flooring

The laminate click–lock prefinished floors can be installed pretty easily in most homes if you have a decent saw and know how to measure. If your floors have more dips and sways than most roller–coasters, or your walls have interesting angles, this isn't the project for a first-time beginner. This type of installation is challenging even for pros.

Tip: you'll save again on labor — it's easier to accomplish if there aren't a lot of doorways, as part of the install involves removing the doors first to perform the job done correctly. Search for "laminate floor installation secrets" on the web.

Shopping

The cheapest price isn't the cheapest if the person ordering isn't accurate or detailed, or forgets to inform you that the faucet will take an extra week after the plumber is already scheduled. The expertise of the person helping you is worth the extra cost (and, as with everything, within reason).

Tools

If you don't have the saws, drills, and other tools needed to do a project, don't forget to factor in their costs when you're calculating your budget. Some of the items, like a wet saw for tile cutting, can be rented, but not all. After all, it's not much of a savings if you spent more on the saw than you would on hiring a pro, *unless you're planning other DIY projects throughout the home.* If that's the case, then here's my next tip. Don't buy cheap tools.

However, if the only tool you have at your disposal is a hammer and you're not planning any other projects, then I might recommend hiring professionals instead. The kitchen is the most expensive room in the home to remodel. Don't spend the money twice as you learn from your mistakes.

A final note — timelines

One of my early readers for this book asked if I could provide an estimate on how much time DIY projects take to accomplish.

That's a tough one. If I had to estimate based on the stories I've heard over the years, I'd calculate that DIY projects take between 2–6 times as long as the work we accomplish with our construction company. Thus, a simple kitchen gut–and–replace (such as glamorous term, isn't it?) and without major structural changes that we can complete in 2–3 months may take 4–18 months for a DIY-er.

Of course, the biggest reasons is that construction is our day job, and not something we have to work on in the evening and on weekends after our day job is over.

It all depends.

—— CHAPTER 5 ——

ASSEMBLING YOUR TEAM
(EVEN IF IT'S ONLY YOU!)

Not a DIY-er?

While I admire those with the DIY skill, desire, and talent, it's safe to say I wasn't blessed with any of them. This business has both spoiled me and made me aware of all the things I'd be doing wrong.

I once spent two weeks painting my walls in my vaulted ceiling home. Never again. My ladder wasn't tall enough, and the extension on the paint roller only stretched so far. You don't want to know what my cut-in lines (that's the delineation of paint where the ceiling and wall meet) at the ceiling looked like. (Well, maybe you do, but I destroyed the evidence.) When I moved out of the place, I saved my pennies and hired a painting crew. They were done within 7 hours. I gave up painting that day.

My tile work in a former powder room was serviceable even if it had a grout line the width of the Mississippi. (At least the grout didn't crack.)

I know there are others out there like me. For those of you who are not DIY-ers, you're probably wondering:

"Where do I find my pros?"
"How do I know the right questions to ask?"
"How do I know who the right one is?"

The joy of remodeling these days is that there are professionals online, with websites, blogs, or even offering suggestions in forums. They're an excellent start for what you're looking for, especially if you've just moved into the area and don't know a soul.

Who should you approach to get the work done?

It's easy to shop for products — you know where to go for appliances, and cabinets, etc. But where do you shop for people to do the work? How do you know who to look for if you don't even know what they do?

Before we start, let me say this: as with every profession in the world, there are both experienced and non–experienced, professional and the not–so–professional, the organized and the messy. *Keep your eyes and ears open, and let's start with the categories:*

1) **Big stores:** In this case, I'm referring to any large regional home im- provement chain store that offers both products and services.

   - **Good for:** One–stop shopping, lots of products to see, accepts credit cards, and are open 7 days a week with some late night shopping hours.

   - **Be aware:** Each store, region, and location varies wildly for service and experience. Services and construction may be outsourced, and skills vary widely. No clearly defined chain–of–command exists between a store and sourced labor, which can cause some degree of heartache if something goes wrong. Pricing is sometimes not any less than a local shop, especially when you start talking higher–end kitchens.

2) **Contractors:** May be sole proprietor who installs all the materials you buy, to a small company who sells and services limited product, to large scale companies with in–house design.

   - **Good for:** Never mind the horror stories you've heard — I'm talking about the hard–working trained professionals I'd work with any day. What you receive is often hands–on service, personal pride in work- manship and skills, someone able to steer you away from mistakes and one point of contact.

   - **Be aware:** Some contractors…aren't. Some never grow or learn new skills. Others can be excellent with their hands, but hate paperwork.

3) **Design/Build firms:** Think of these as a contractor with showrooms, designers, and crew under one roof. The designs they come up with, they also build. They may have architects or designers on staff, and/or may supply or recommend products.

- **Good for:** Personal service, better–than–average kitchen design, possibly certified or licensed designers on staff or be architect–led. Level of detail is typically high. You will have help every step of the way and the lines of communication are strong.
- **Be aware:** Not open all hours like retail stores. Some present entire start–to–finish packages without providing full breakdowns of every item. Skill level varies but this time on the higher side, which might result in higher rates.

4) **Independent designers:** Some may supply design and plan services only; others may order products. Some specialize in kitchen design; others are general practitioners.

- **Good for:** Helping you sort out your vision and come up with a plan to make everything fit. Have the experience with the products and materials to help you select in a fraction of the time it would take you on your own. The truly experienced will spot and eliminate problems before you start and really make you think about all the ramifications of your choices.
- **Be aware:** Not all specialize in kitchen design. If they don't understand construction or have the experience to deal with product quirks, they could create some serious challenges during construction. Their hours are typically by appointment. You'll still need to hire a contractor and/or architect unless they are a general contractor or architect as well.

5) **Architects:** Some may supply drafting services only; others prefer to oversee your entire project for a fixed fee or a percentage of the construction costs. The partner (or leading architect) may start the project and design but pass the actual drafting to someone else in the office with lesser ability (and a smaller hourly rate). This is very common but

it makes more economic sense to the client regardless of the way the fee is scheduled (hourly versus fixed fee).

- **Good for:** Concise plans, clearly laid-out details, a clear vision from start to finish on every aspect of design detail. They have the vision and experience of designing exteriors and additions, which most designers do not. They also have the experience for dealing with planning departments on set-backs and variances, environmental conditions, and construction details.
- **Be aware:** With apologies to the architects I know, some architects are more about vision than budget. While architects are good at the latest building practices, they might not be current on the latest finish products or appliances.

6) **Handymen:** A good handyman is great for the smaller projects and for the Reluctant Remodeler who is faced with a fixer-upper such as adding new trim work or a backsplash or two.

- **Good for:** Smaller one-time projects, especially if you're not a DIY-er. Some are extremely experienced for all kinds of small projects.
- **Be aware:** Some don't place enough importance on good communication or paperwork detail; some don't have enough training.

7) **Lumberyards:** I have a lot of affection for the lumberyards. They're the last old time holdout from the days of hardware stores and personal service. Some have gone extremely personal and upscale — others still cater to the trade. In many cases, most have a cabinet center, along with good cabinet people, and sometimes even a full design service. (I was once asked to take over the cabinet representation for a group of lumberyards. The cabinet line was a line you'd see in designer showrooms anywhere.)

- **Good for:** Small one-off items, such as a piece of molding, or one cabinet, or a handle, or a sink. I liken lumberyards (depending on the lumberyard, of course) as the midpoint between the convenience of a big box store with the personalization and service of a smaller shop.
- **Be aware:** The kitchen section is only as good as the designers or the person specifying.

Many of these trades work together, such as an architect bringing a kitchen designer on board, or interior designers recommending contractors they respect or a lumber yard supplying cabinets to a contractor. This isn't meant to be the definitive list, but to give you an idea of the possibilities.

Hiring a contractor

Again, I'm aware I come from a different background. I grew up and worked with professional and ethical contractors. The very few bad eggs I met over the early years truly shocked me, but I've certainly heard enough stories over the years, as well as worked with clients who were taken advantage of, that I realize it's buyer beware. I hate hearing stories about people getting taken advantage of, or work being performed poorly, but I'm also indignant for the hard-working professional contractors who constantly battle against the perception that all contractors are the same. They're not. Like everybody else, contractors come with varying skill sets, and knowledge.

Before the referrals, and friend recommendations, here is what I think should be the standard for anyone looking for a contractor (also colloquially known as a builder when building a home and not remodeling):

a) a business license

b) an actual office (even if it is in a home)

c) a business phone (not just a cell phone)

Anyone can make a business card. Anyone can have a truck. You need someone who has spent the money to establish a place that says, "Yes, I'm here." Having local business licenses is also a step in the right direction.

Never do business without a contract
It doesn't matter if it's a tile-setter laying tile, or a contractor building your home—a contract spells out the work, provides both parties with reasonable expectation of the work provided, and, in the case of a dispute, can help resolve it. Protect yourself.

You notice I didn't mention the contractor's license. Yes, they should have one. The number should usually be posted on all correspondence. What most people do is look at the number and think, "Good. They have a contractor's license", and don't check its legitimacy.

The fly–by–nighters and scam artists, as well as the lazy who shouldn't be in the business, all bank on you not checking. And, unfortunately, it's a scam that works and is usually not discovered until it's too late. They make it tough for the rest. A licensed contractor wants you to check him or her out, trust me. They don't like scammers any more than you do.

Go online to your state licensing board. Check to see if your contractor there. Good. Now check to see that the name of the contractor matches the person you're talking to. Why? If someone doesn't have a number, they might have "borrowed" someone else's for their work. Whether they had permission or not, if something goes wrong, they're not on the hook for the problem, the other contractor is — and that's usually where the finger–pointing and delays in resolution come in. You want the person who has the license to stand behind their name or the company's name.

Hiring a Kitchen Designer

Long before I started this book, I kept hearing a common thread: "How can I find a *good* designer?"

I couldn't figure that one out. After all, I communicate with quite a few in forums, meetings, and online everyday!

Feel free to mock me, because it's an important distinction and I was slow to understand.

What you're really saying is you want someone who not only understands the nuances of design but who also understands you — your lifestyle, your family, and what's important to you in the creation of this new space.

From my viewpoint, you also need a designer who understands both safety and function, plus the longevity of the products based on your lifestyle. Is the floor too slippery for a baker who spills flour on the floor? Will the drawer open next to the dishwasher if it has a larger handle? Will the corner of the island be too sharp for the 4–year–old racing around the room?

Here's when hiring a designer is a good idea.
- When you don't have any idea what you're doing and/or don't have time or inclination, and don't want to make a mistake.

- When you're changing the layout.
- When you're planning on custom anything — custom appliances, cabinets, lighting, etc. can quadruple the mistake level of a simple gut-and-replace.
- When you know nothing about design.
- When you don't have time to oversee the plan.
- When you need help with coordinating colors, or finishes, or styles.

Here's when hiring a designer isn't necessary.
- When you're changing out one or two items, such as a sink or refrigerator.
- When your existing architect, or contractor, or interior designer has experience in the kitchen. They'll tell you if they don't.
- When you're pretty comfortable with your own design, color choices, and style.

How much does a designer cost? — Depending on the designer's experience, costs run from $50.00 per hour for a newer designer to $200.00 per hour and up for an experienced or well-known designer.

Some might have package rates for full or partial design, while others' work might be included in the price of a complete remodel. Don't be afraid to ask: "What are your design fees?"

If you're a DIY–er and want a second opinion but lack the design budget, perhaps paying for an hour for a designer to look over your design for any flaws might be a very inexpensive form of insurance, especially if he or she finds something that is wrong or could be improved on.

Let's talk about the different types of kitchen designers

There are designers who own a home business or a showroom, and those, like me, who work for an independent business. Some will supply products, or specialize in design services only, or have combinations of both. I know wonderful freelance designers who believe that anyone who sells product is compromised, and others who prefer to work with tried-and-tested products they can stand behind. Some designers have taken every known course; other designers have a 3-day cabinet seminar under their belts.

So, the question becomes, what do you want from your designer? Are you planning a full remodel, or replacing the cabinets only? Do you want him or her to steer you clear of mistakes? Inform you of the latest, perhaps green products? Do you want to hire them for a couple of hours? For a consultation? Or do you want them to handle your entire project?

There is no one answer. If you simply want design help, look for a freelance designer or a design company that does just that.

If you're looking for someone to co-ordinate the styles and colors of your kitchen, dining room, hallway — then look to a designer who's part of a design team or design/build team.

If you're looking for help for an entire kitchen gut, then look to construction companies, or interior design companies who have their own network of contractors and subcontractors to make things happen. In this case, you're looking for an experienced kitchen designer, an interior designer with kitchen experience, or someone who's a mixture of both. Then interview them.

Designers expect to be interviewed. We like meeting people and hearing about their projects. We don't expect to hit it off with every person, but, like you, we're also looking for a good fit too.

Also, don't be afraid to contact the designers you've admired in magazines and/or on television. There's a perception that they are all too expensive. Some are, but many aren't. (If they're single-named designer or otherwise well-known, chances are he or she might consume a large part of your design budget!)

Interviewing potential designers

Remember what I said about good and bad contractors? The same goes for designers.

Ever wondered what you should be looking for in your designer?

The good signs:
- They listen to you. I mean, really listen. Doesn't that sound odd? But I'm amazed at how many designers don't let the consumer get a word in edge-wise, especially new designers. Please forgive them. They're excited about all the neat stuff they have and are so happy to show you, they forget you'd like a chance to be excited too. (I think back to my puppy years and cringe. I'm sorry, people-whose-ears-I-talked-off.)
- You communicate well with each other. Sometimes, there are people that you don't connect with. That's life. You say "a" and the other person hears "b" and vice-versa. It's not bad or wrong, other than a difference in communication, but when it happens, it can lead to mistakes and dissatisfaction. It's why I say, "So what I'm hearing you say is this... Is that correct?" If we can't connect by the second meeting, I'm not the designer for them. However, when you that good vibe energy from the very beginning, it's the best feeling in the world.

They provide clear reasons and good answers to your questions.

Designers expect you to test them — at least the experienced ones do — and they're comfortable with it. How do you know how much experience a person has, if you don't ask? A designer should also be able to articulate very clearly the reason why a product does or does not work, not simply tell you that it is or isn't "good".

The warning signs are:
- You can't get a word in edgewise.
- Your ideas are ignored or brushed off without explanation.
- Paperwork isn't organized.
- Calls aren't returned in a timely manner.
- They're pushing their ideas without providing reasons.

Pay attention to your gut feelings, but also be practical. Sometimes, it's simply not a good fit. Recognize when meeting with your designer doesn't make you happy that it's time for a frank discussion or to call it quits.

Also don't forget to ask the designers about their experience, their designations, what license they practice under (or if they have a license), and what their terms are.

A note on trades working together

Every once in awhile there are trades that don't work well together — contractors who don't think a designer knows anything about construction, or a designer who thinks trades are minions instead of part of the team, or architects who believe they're the only ones with brains on a project. It takes some time to build a team, to find those who know (and appreciate) how you think, who are interested in building a team with you, and who like the synergy of working together.

It's important to discover if your architect is willing to work with your interior designer, or if your contractor wants to meet with your kitchen designer. In my opinion, you need to get these people in the same room to see how they can work together before they start. You don't want (and shouldn't need) to play the parent during your project, yet I've seen it happen many, many times.

Personally, I find those who are extremely experienced and knowledgeable to be the most professional and best to work with — in all fields. They're secure in what they do, and appreciate everyone's input, even if they don't take it.

I was taught that the mark of a leader is to be willing to accept responsibility for his or her mistakes. Find those that feel the same way. True professional collaboration creates energy and joy that is truly inspiring to be a part of.

The rebel approach for getting the right quotes for you

You know the old adage: "Get three quotes?"

I might suggest tossing it out the window, unless you're doing the most basic of designs, and are shopping for individual items, like cabinetry (and even then, there are some caveats). Oh, sure, you can say, "But I want this style cabinet, and this flooring and this lighting. What's so hard?"

It's not simply about buying products, it's about the skill level, expertise and knowledge of the people installing them. It's not enough to simply look at the numbers and judge everything on that. Stories abound of people who don't do their homework.

The questions to ask when checking referrals:

a) Was the project completed in a timely manner or when the contractor/ designer/tradesperson said?
b) If not, was it beyond their control or because items were added?
c) Was the site kept tidy, or at least kept clean throughout the life of the project?
d) Were all the people who worked for your contractor competent?
e) Were there any problems? How were they handled? This one is *important* — there will be at least one challenge that pops up. How it's dealt with will give you some insight.

Bring pictures so everyone's on board

If you don't know exactly what you want, your prices will vary all over the place based on each person's vision.

Let's use tile backsplash as an example. What does it mean when you say you want a fancy backsplash? To me, it means high–end tiles, at least 3 or 4 in varying sizes and shapes, and multiple design challenges to be worked out to get the pieces right. To others, it might mean using a stock tile and inserting a decorative tile every so often. One is a quarter of the cost in both tile and the time to set them.

In our design/build firm, I rely on different tile setters for different projects. Some are great at simple one–tile–with–a–border backsplashes and their prices reflect that — but asking them to install a complex five–tile project with multiple tile sizes, types, and thicknesses is beyond their skill level. Using them for price will end up costing us all in delays, re–ordering and dissatisfaction. No, I'm going to use the tile setter with the skills and experience to do the job right — and, yes, it's going to cost more.

Not every plumber can install high–end plumbing fixtures, not all tile setters can work with glass tiles, not every installer knows what to do with a European integrated refrigerator. All of these items add multiple hours.

These very things will trip up the project can cause needless frustration as the person who swore they could install them spends hours scratching his or her head.

I used to joke that the person who's quick to say, "No problem" is the one we have the most problem with. I've found many of the folks who do skilled work tend to hesitate, offer a disclaimer ("It'll take a bit of work, but it's do–able") and/or offer suggestions. As always, your mileage may vary. *The skill is also in the small details and how they will be handled.*

a) Do you know what style of switch plates your contractor will supply? (Decora rocker plates are more expensive than standard toggle.)

b) Is the grout for the tile epoxy or standard?

c) Will anyone check for water damage at the sink wall of your 40–year–old kitchen and add new insulation, or are they going to simply do the most basic reinstallation of your new sink and call it quits? (The professional way in a remodel is to check and correct. A water leak over time is costly.)

d) Is your kitchen designer supplying a 3½" crown molding, or none at all? (Something that can add $1,000–$3,000 to a project). Do they have any knowledge of building to help you understand what will happen with installation in your very crooked 90–year–old house?

Here's what is happening in mid–to–high end design: Twenty years ago, it would take a designer or contractor anywhere from one to four hours to come up with a quote, because there weren't that many products or design styles. Kitchens were easy. You want a quote? No problem.

Today, it takes any contractor, architect, design/build firm, interior designer weeks to quote a large–scale project. Yes, you read that right, weeks. There are quotes for specialty counters, the cabinet design, the flooring, and the backsplash. The electrician and the plumber and other trades visit the home, especially older homes, and understand the grade of lighting you want to install.

All that work takes time, and the good people don't work for free. You'll be paying for at least some of the time and effort it takes to come up with a detailed proposal.

So what do you do?

You don't get quotes, you interview people and business — how they work, what their past records are. If you're reading this and saying, "But I'm not getting high-end, Kelly. Are you saying I shouldn't get quotes?"

No. What I'm saying is that you have to do your homework too and come to the table prepared.

Otherwise, here's the scenario: You've picked three contractors. You've explained you wanted maple cabinets, granite counters, and new appliances in the bid. They come back with their quotes: $12,500.00, $28,000.00, $39,500.00.

What does that tell you? Absolutely nothing. It's like asking travel agencies to price out a 7–day trip to Tahiti without specifying the mode of travel (sure, you said "flight", not boat, but does that mean coach, business, or first class?), the expectations of the hotel rooms (on the water or no sea view?), and the entertainment (flight around the island or rent–a–car?)

<u>Left to their own devices, everyone will price based on their business models.</u>

The first company deals with price — he or she doesn't know the quality difference and doesn't care. He heard you say, "Sharpen your pencil" and that's what he's going to do. He'll select a cabinet that looks good because they all look the same to him, not because of the quality. He'll install three can lights "because you don't need the rest", and the backsplash will be 4" high "because that's what all his clients want." His idea of good appliances is one–step up from rental.

The second heard you say, "I'd like a custom maple cabinet", and prices a mid–range semi–custom line. He has a good sense of your neighborhood, knows what the homes have for like quality (including adding the pot drawers and other options), will add the six can lights and the full–height tile backsplash. He also came up with a design that is better than what you started with, and priced in decent, mid–range appliances.

The third heard you say, "I'd like a custom maple cabinet" and gave you a true custom maple cabinet with all the bells and whistles, some high–end appliances, and completely worked the design to give you everything you asked for and even some of the design aspects you hadn't.

See where I'm going with this?

There's a better way

Don't price in the beginning.

It won't help you in the beginning when you're not even sure what you want, and it'll save everyone a lot of time.

Visit or call the people you're interested in.

That means looking through their website or visiting their showrooms. Look at their portfolio. If you see something you like or find a layout similar to your new vision, then call them and ask the approximate cost of the kitchens closest in layout to yours. Don't panic or dismiss anyone at this stage if the costs don't match what you thought. It's too early yet, and you're looking for more than price.

If the range they tell you is higher than you expect, ask where you could save money.

Or ask them if they've done similar projects at a lower investment range. Tell them you're in the preliminary stages of selecting your team and will contact them if you need anything further.

Now narrow your choices, and interview them.

This is still without asking for a price for your project (unless you've been planning this for 5 years and know every detail. You're ahead of most people who are starting). Look at the projects they've done. Look for someone who understands the properties of your selections, has the expertise and training to help you, and matches your expectations. Call the references, and check out the company credentials. Don't simply rely on a neighbor telling you Acme Company did a good job. This is your kitchen. Research, research, research.

When you've done some more research, compile a list.

Say you want a cabinet that's similar in quality to X Brand. List the options. Say you want six can lights, and the tile you want to use will be similar to Y Brand. Show them the tile design you like.

Don't get three quotes, get two.

You're not narrowing it down to cost; you're narrowing it down to who you want to work with. Now you're really comparing paperwork detail, which can sometimes be every bit as important as the project itself.

When comparing the prices, ask what's not included in the price.

Are they taking care of the permits? Will they clean up afterwards? Is there crown molding? Is the appliance installation included? (In the higher end appliances, manufacturers honor the warranties only if you use one of their licensed installers.)

A *final caveat:* in the higher–end design, some firms provide an overall price without cost breakdowns. Yes, they might provide different options based on product choices, but it's a different market. If this sounds like putting too much trust in a company, look to how long they've been a company. They're expected to perform at a higher level of quality, and their reputations and word–of–mouth make or break them. Their clients expect them to perform to a certain high standard, and they usually do. The price is secondary to the quality and level of detail.

If you come away from this thinking, "This is a lot of work", you're right. But pair the right team with your kitchen ideas and you'll discover how much easier it'll be.

PART 3

THE INSIDER SECRETS FOR MAKING YOUR KITCHEN WORK

CHAPTER 6

CABINETS TIPS AND TRICKS

Basic kitchen design isn't rocket science, but there are kitchen planning tips and tricks to make the actual construction of the project easier. Everything has its own quirks — knowing them is half the battle.

Cabinet design can be fairly costly in both time and money if one is missing any details and needs to re-order. It's also the one area where people are so focused on the layout, they often forget the other elements that hinder or obstruct the cabinetry installation until it's too late.

We're going to look at an extensive checklist of these common and some of the not-so-common oversights. Even if you're not ordering the cabinets yourself, you might find the lists helpful to understand what you're getting.

If you have a rough plan or some ideas already fleshed out, great. See if there's anything in here you missed.

A tip on avoiding sticker shock

At one time, cabinets were built to accommodate the appliances. They were built in-house, without any interior options. It made it easy to quote because a few sheets of plywood, some hinges, and some knobs, and you could literally estimate a run of cabinets. In fact, some people still ask for cabinet quotes this way: "What's the cost of this cabinet per foot?"

Today's kitchens simply have too many options and styles for this method to work any more. But to walk into a showroom and pick something because you like it and then discover that it's far above what you planned to spend is a common occurrence. How will you know where to add and scale back if you've never had to face this before? And how do you avoid sticker shock?

I've got a few ideas.

Pricing cabinets is like papier–mâché

At least, this is how I explain the concept to my clients. The wire–frame (design) is the starting point. Each layer of paper (the options) adds another layer of thickness (costs).

The best way to keep the budget intact is to understand what the cost is of adding each individual layer. But what are they?

1) **Options:** Without a doubt, these are the "super–sizing" of our industry. Add special glazing to a door vs. a standard stain, a special ogee counter edge vs. a plainer edge, or a custom backsplash tile vs. none. Each one on its own isn't dangerous to a budget, but they have a cumulative effect you need to know before you finalize the details. Even the options have their own options these days!

   Take a roll–out shelf in a pantry, for example. Would you prefer:
   a) ¾–extension glides or full–extension glides?
   b) Standard closing or soft–closing hardware?
   c) Plain melamine boxes or wood furniture boxes with dovetail joints?

   They all pull out so that the items on the shelf easier to reach. How far they pull out and what degree of window dressing adds the extra cost.

Budget saver — stay with standard: Start here first. Learn what your upgrades, add–ons, or options are and their costs. If the budget needs to be trimmed, you'll know where.

---

2) **Good design:** A kitchen filled with 12"–15"wide cabinets is more expensive than a kitchen with fewer cabinets that are 24"–30" wide — and

also less useful. Or any design which causes a door to hit against a door or obstructs an appliance from opening will be costly to fix during the construction stage. I can't recommend enough in laying out the plan on graph paper with all the door swings and drawer openings. The elevations will show the width and heights of the doors. This is one of the best ways to tune and re–tune.

3) **Labor:** Anything that veers from straight and simple takes longer to install and cost more money. Staggered cabinet heights and depths, custom size doors and panels, fancy tile backsplashes, or multiple lighting sources are all good examples of adding extra to your project.

This is why the same kitchen layout can vary thousands of dollars. As soon as you add the specialty lighting, intricate floor and wall designs, fancy moldings around windows and doors — all the bright and shiny items that you want — you've experienced scope creep.

Sticker shock isn't uncommon. Education of all aspects of the project is absolutely necessary.

Do your base cabinets have full–depth shelves?
Some cabinet manufacturers offer only partial shelves as a way to cut costs. The upside is that it's easier to reach above and below the half–depth shelf; the downside is that half a storage shelf is lost. Ask for the cabinet construction page to verify the depth.

Insider Definitions

Before we start with the tips, let's clarify some designer and regional jargon not covered in the "Insider Definition" sidebars. Even though some terms are standard throughout the design and construction industry, some terms are regional — remodeling vs. renovation, for example.

Hopefully, you won't receive blank stares when you use them; if you do, refer to the translations below:

a) **Door Swings:** Something I use frequently instead of "opens" or "opening", as in "check your door swings." A right–hand swing means as you face the cabinet, the hinges are on the right, and the handle is on the left (the door swings open to the right), and vice versa.

b) **Gable or side panel:** A gable is simply a regional term for a side panel, whether it refers to the side of a cabinet or to a base or refrigerator panel.

c) **Bind:** When a drawer or door won't open because they are restricted in some way, either by a crooked wall, or an improper installation, or a handle. As in, "The right swing door is binding against the dishwasher. We'll need to change it to a left–hand swing."

Let's start by looking at the two construction styles of cabinetry, framed vs. frameless.

Frame vs. Frameless cabinets

A framed cabinet may also be called a "traditional" or "face frame" cabinet. The front opening of the cabinet has a frame, which is 1½" wide, fitted over the opening of the cabinet, hence the name. <u>The hinges of a frame cabinet are mounted on the frame</u>. This is an older style compared to the frameless cabinet.

A frameless or European cabinet doesn't have this frame. <u>The hinges are mounted on the interior side wall of the cabinet</u>. I was taught that frameless cabinets were invented by the Germans after the Second World War due to a lack of building materials and wood supplies.

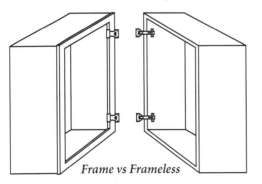

Sometimes you can't tell the difference between the two cabinets when you go shopping, but if you open a door and check the hinges, they'll tell you the cabinet style every time.

Frame vs Frameless

Why is the difference important?

Each cabinet requires different installation techniques. Frameless cabinets aren't nailed; they're pre-drilled first and then screwed to the walls and each other. The cabinet boxes must be plumb and square no matter how the walls, floors, and ceilings wander. This is what most beginners, DIY or not, don't know.

If you simply install a frameless box on a crooked wall, the cabinet may twist or "rack" and, in turn, twist the doors. You'll never be able to straighten them, no matter how much they're adjusted, and the only solution will be to remove and re-install the cabinet properly by adding shims behind (and under the cabinet) to level the walls and floors. Or actually leveling the walls, floors, and ceilings before you start, but that can become very costly.

Framed cabinets are more forgiving, which may make them more appropriate for some DIY projects. Some can be nailed (although using screws are better), and the extra trims and fillers that space frameless cabinets away from a door frame or a corner may already be part of a framed cabinet. They still need to be screwed together, so having some degree of level and square is still important.

If you're using an installer, the most important requirement is to make sure the installer you hire is familiar with both. An installer of ours, who was quite talented with framed cabinets, still required some advice on his first frameless cabinet install. Whether you are using an installer or not, it might be less stressful if you or your installer has experience with the type of cabinets you'll purchase.

Cabinet heights

The majority of homes from 1980s and earlier in North America have 8' or 96" high ceilings. Older apartments, condos, pre-War units may have 10'-12' ceilings. Newer homes may have 9' or even higher, but for now, let's consider the 8' ceilings because they're the most common and pose the most height challenges. *Unless you're dealing with custom cabinets, most stock and semi-custom cabinetry lines contain the following heights:*

a) **Kitchen base cabinets:** 34"–35" high. With a 1½" high counter, the final height should be at 36" or close to it.

b) **Desk or office cabinets:** 30"h–36"h

c) **Wall cabinets:** 30" high, 36" high and 42" high. (Some also are 39" high or may be a variation of the above. i.e. 35" high.)

d) **Tall cabinets:** 84" high (which correspond with 30" high wall cabinets), 90" high (36" high wall cabinets) and 96" (42" high wall cabinets).

Most of these cabinets come in 3" wide increments and can come in the following applications:

a) **True stock cabinet:** No modifications. What you see in the brochure is what you get.

b) **Flat pack:** Usually stock. You assemble the cabinets yourself (or pay someone to assemble them for you.

c) **Semi-custom cabinet:** This is a big range and varies anywhere from a cabinet line that only allows for changes in cabinet depth (because the doors are a fixed size) to a line that allows for quite a bit of customization of boxes, drawers, and other details. For me, if the door sizing can't be altered for width or height, that's a stock cabinet. I'm old school.

d) **True Custom:** Now you're talking anything you want for cabinets, trims, and special details. This may be a factory line, and can also be a skilled woodworker crafting the cabinets in your home.

Again, if you've never installed cabinetry before and you have a home that has uneven floors and out-of-square walls, I would strongly advise hiring a cabinet installer. Of course, if it's your dream to try it yourself, have fun!

"We Have Doughnuts" — How to write your measurements right

Before you think I've lost my marbles, let me explain. There is an industry standard for writing measurements, whether you're ordering cabinets, doors, or windows (or anything else). Getting them in the wrong order will hurt, in more ways than you can imagine — and you'll end up with the wrong product. Measurements are listed as: width, height, and depth. Since I could never remember in the early years, here's the way I got it to stick:

> ("**We Have Doughnuts**" = **Width, Height, Depth**)

Most beginners, including order takers, get this wrong. If you don't follow what the standard rules are, there's bound to be some mix–up that isn't going to come out in your favor.

It doesn't hurt to list a 21"×30"×12" cabinet as: 21"w by 30"h by 12"d. (Or you can use an '×' between the numbers, which also stands for "by" (21"w × 30"h × 12"d)

Here's how to read and write the cabinet configurations on a cabinet layout:

a) **Wall cabinets:** Using the number above of 21"×30"×12", a typical wall cabinet is written W2130. Wall cabinets are presumed to be 12" deep unless otherwise stated.

b) **Base cabinets:** A typical 24" wide base is written as a B24. Base cabinets don't list the height or depth unless it has a special depth. An example of a custom base would be a B241240 — a base unit which is 24" wide × 12" deep × 40" high.

c) **Tall cabinets:** Tall cabinets usually list all three number — an ST302490 is a storage cabinet that's 30"w by 24" deep × 90" high.

All single–door cabinets are labeled with an "L" (left) or "R" (right) to indicate which side the hinges are mounted. Pretend you're facing the cabinet. The hinging is indicated when placing a cabinet order.

Two common myths about cabinets

1. *"Dovetail drawer boxes are a sign of quality and are better than other drawer construction"* — Dovetail drawer boxes are a leftover from over 100 years ago when not everyone had nails at their disposal. Most cabinets were held together with a combination of joints such as dovetails, and, in some cases, horsehair glue.

2. *"Particleboard cabinets are cheap"* — No, the good quality construction board is not. Just as there are multiple grades of plywood, there are multiple grades of particle or construction

board. A company who strives for a sturdy product uses a 38–to 42–pound 3–layer composition board, which holds a screw and doesn't break apart. I've seen both cheap plywood and cheap particleboard. High quality and long–lasting cabinetry uses neither.

"Tree" facts you should know about wood doors

If you want cabinets built out of wood and prefer them perfectly clear and free of blemishes, marks, or different graduations of grain, be prepared to pay for it (this is what I think of when someone says "cherry" picking — one needs to buy double or more of a batch in order to pick amongst them for the clearest pieces), or forget wood entirely and buy laminate or painted instead. The beauty in wood is in its graining, and as my father was fond of saying, "You can't tell a tree how to grow."

Even if the wood was all logged from the same batch of forest, here's why they'll never be the same:

- One tree grew in the shade.
- One grew in the sun.
- One grew at the bottom of the hill and the other at the top.
- One received more water than the others while others suffered during a drought.

Any and all of these affect the tree, and the wood you're buying. The little dark patches on panels are mineral streaks, which are an integral part of many woods and definitely not a flaw (unless the faces are covered worse than a kid with measles.) Tiny pin–knots and changes of the grain are also acceptable, and are all dependent on the tree, the farming, the milling, the grading, and finally, the quality level of the cabinets you're buying.

Wood changes color over time

All woods change color as they age, but cherry and exotic woods change the most within the first 3–6 months. Other woods that show visible changes are fir, cedar, and pine. With these woods, it's important to select your colors using a door sample that has already

> aged, and to understand that the colors will look slightly "off" when
> the cabinets are first installed until the wood finally ages.

Unless you're paying for a cabinet that has "premium" or "select", expect some variations.

Wood is living long after it's installed. It "moves" — swells when there's a great deal of humidity in the air and shrinks when the air is arid. It's why few make a "solid" door out of one piece of wood — the grain may cause the door to warp. Most wood doors are made in a butcher block pattern, with a loose center panel to adapt to these changes in humidity.

In low–humidity areas such as Arizona, a door can dry out so much that the pieces shrink, exposing the unstained edges of the center panel. Or the pieces will look like they're separating. If humidity is restored to the room, then the door swells back to its normal size and the stain or paint line goes away.

Knowing the characteristics of the wood, how it will age, and what the maintenance requirements are before you order will go a long way to choosing cabinets you're happy about in the long run.

A note on the darker stains and thin center panels
Plywood sometimes stains differently than solid woods,
especially the darker the stain is. If you're planning a Shaker
door style where the recessed center panel is a thin piece of
plywood, the recessed center panel will stain differently
than the frame. If this is not what you want, then you want
a center panel that is made out of solid wood.
Really study the samples before you buy.

Painted cabinets

Painted cabinets use wood, construction board, or a combination of both. Depending on where you live, the perceived value of quality will fall into either category. *Here are the two viewpoints:*

1) **Painted finishes on wood:**

   (Note: for now I'm talking simply paint. Some companies use a pigmented stain.) The reasons people select painted wood are:
   - It's a traditional look that has been around for generations. Depending on the wood type, the cabinets will have some imperfections. They might show as a bump over a knot, or show dimpled dents.
   - They like the variations. The wood, as it expands and contracts may show cracks in the paint finish at all joints.

2) **Painted finishes on construction board:**

   The reason people select painted fiberboard (also known as MDF — medium density fiberboard) is:
   - They prefer a clean, smooth finish. Fiberboard doesn't expand or contract which ensures all joints are smooth. The surface might have a slight pebbly look depending on the fiberboard used.

Those in the painted wood camp have a difficult time understanding those who'd like "an automotive finish with no character"; those in the fiberboard camp wonder why anyone "would want cracked paint finishes?"

I say whatever makes you happy — either one is going to stand the test of time.

The only time where it might make a difference is with door panels mounted on appliance doors — MDF is heavier than many woods. Most appliances specifications list an allowable weight level. Exceed that level and you're in danger of overloading the door springs. This is a case–by–case scenario, as I've certainly installed many MDF painted panels on appliances, but there has been one or two over the years where I wouldn't have recommended the MDF panels.

Thermofoil doors

Thermofoil looks like paint, but isn't. It's a plastic liner glued and heat–formed onto a fiberboard and was meant as a less expensive successor to painted cabinets. It doesn't wrap around the entire door, but is formed in two pieces, one that covers the front and wraps around the edges, and one that covers the back of the door. (The cheaper thermofoil doors may not even have this backing — they'll use a less-expensive plastic coating instead.) Quality ranges across the board, from the glossy Italian thermofoils at the top of the price range down to some "won't-last-a-day" bargain specials.

The pro of thermofoil is the cost, and like everything, you get what you pay for. The con is that the cheaper material can take more work to clean; it can burn, and — with the right amount of steam and the wrong door, can delaminate at the edges.

With proper care, the majority of cabinets will last years.

Other door styles

There are others out on the market today — laminate doors in hundreds of shades which are both durable and cost-effective, stainless which are more industrial and costly, and resin-covered doors, which may have a high-gloss polyurethane over the foil or paint cover.

With the exception of the laminate doors, the others tend to be custom and not usually found in factory cabinet lines.

When does it make sense to reface instead of replace?

Re-facing cabinets — covering the exposed areas with a new material, such as a laminate or wood skin — is another way to change the old, out-dated look of your kitchen.

These days, re-facing can also mean replacing the doors and drawers only, while leaving the cabinet frames and boxes in place. It doesn't work well for every kitchen, especially those whose older cabinet frames are falling apart.

Here are a couple of thoughts: If you're planning on replacing the countertop in a few years, seriously hold off on the re-facing, especially if you're in it for the long term.

At one time, depending on materials and possible labor for replacing drawer glides or hinges, there wasn't a lot of cost difference between re-facing and basic new cabinets. Consider pricing out new cabinets and comparing the costs before you make a final decision.

If you say to me, "But, Kelly, I can't stand the cabinets and I need to update them now," and the budget won't do much more, here's how to make the best possible choice.

Re-face when:

The cabinets are in relatively good shape.

That means the frames aren't falling apart, and in the case of actually re-facing the existing surfaces with another material, that the doors and drawers don't have chunks or gouges.

The original cabinets are sturdy.

If the doors are falling off, or the drawer glides no longer function well, or the cabinet itself is made of poor quality materials — think very cheap raw construction board with no protective coatings — then you could be throwing your money away. Eventually the cabinets will have to be replaced sooner than you think. What's the use of spending the money now to replace the counter and doors, only to discover the frame is rotting away a few years later?

The hinge and hinge holes aren't worn out.

This is a variation of the point above. I've seen re-facing where the new doors fell off the cabinets as soon as they were completed because the company reinstalled the hinges and screws over the stripped screw holes. A good re-facing company will either add new wood (called a block or blocking) for the new screws, or install the hinges either above or below the existing screw holes. If the hinges are all screwed tight to the doors and frames and haven't moved in years, then it might not be an issue.

There are few cabinet doors and doors.

A mid-sized kitchen here has between 24–30 doors and 10–14 drawer fronts, which can really add up if you're replacing every one of them and why I suggest pricing both re-facing and new cabinets. It's certainly more reasonable on the budget if you have a smaller kitchen.

Finally, check the references of the company doing the project, and how long they've been in business.

I might suggest asking for older references along with the newer ones, to see how well the work has stood the test of time.

Regional note: *Factory–finished panels won't hide the gap between the crooked wall and the back of the cabinet and the wall; your cabinet will need an extra piece of wood trim or molding installed to cover the gap between the back of the straight cabinet and the imperfection of the wall. Where I grew up, using this trim was Not Done—one ordered the panels loose and cut the back of the panel to follow the waves in the wall (called "scribing"). Where I am now, factory–finished panels and trim are perfectly acceptable. Your mileage may vary.*

Order up! The top 11 beginner mistakes of cabinetry orders (and how to avoid them)

1) **Tearing out your kitchen before the cabinets are even ordered.** Don't be caught with the "hurry–up–and–wait" crowd. It takes time to order. Most cabinets take anywhere from 4–8 weeks from order to delivery. For a cabinet–maker, it depends on the materials, layout, and design, while luxury or custom cabinets can take 10–18 weeks or more.

2) **Not ordering enough trim.** It's never a good idea to get stingy on your moldings. While you might think you're saving money, it won't be much of a savings if your installer has to wait another couple of weeks for a new piece. Also, some moldings may contain knots or slight imperfections which need to be cut out, or the saw blade might slip. It happens. Here's the trick: count an extra 6" per corner that the molding has to wrap around. Most moldings are 96" long. Be generous.

3) **Not realizing that cabinets are made (and shipped) in separate pieces.** We recently had a client who was upset when the island he ordered from us came as six separate cabinets. He was expecting a complete 6'×4' island ready to be set in his kitchen. Unless your cabinets are a higher-end cabinet line or your cabinet-maker can make them the way you want, it's up to you and/or your contractor to assemble these pieces.

4) **Didn't pay attention to the size of cabinet doors.** It looks better when the cabinet doors are similar in size. Tiny and overly large doors aren't as useful. I call it the Goldilocks guideline of cabinet design.

   Too big: 24" wide doors — the door will swing out over the counter into your work space. — **Too small:** 9" or 12" doors or smaller. Sometimes, we need one or two, but a roomful is truly annoying — **Just right:** 15"–21" wide.

The Goldilocks rule for arched or cathedral door styles
On a 9" wide door, an arch resembles a pinched inchworm. The inchworm flattens on a 21" door. (How do you like those visuals? You're welcome!) Too much variation looks busy.

5) **Didn't realize that the sides, tops or bottoms of cabinets aren't finished unless specified.** Cabinets are not finished the same as the rest of the cabinet face — they may be white (when your cabinet is wood) or vice versa. If there's a breakfast nook or table in the kitchen, chances are you'll see the underside of the wall cabinets when seated. Under-cabinet light rail or trim may hide some of this, but if bothers you, figure on adding some under cabinet panels for the areas you do see. Some of you won't care; others will be thinking of their white cabinet boxes with their dark cherry doors, and making a quick trip to the store.

Hide the unfinished underside of your refrigerator cabinet:
If your refrigerator isn't built–in, chances are you'll see the underside of the cabinet above it. Not all cabinet lines offer a finished bottom on a cabinet. Another solution is to order a length of valance material which can be installed under the cabinet doors to hide much of the unfinished bottom.

6) **Ordering a lazy susan after the cabinet is installed.** Almost impossible to install after the countertop is installed — any I've seen are usually so small that they're not efficient. Best time to decide is *before* you order.

7) **The glass door cabinet interior doesn't match the exterior.** Cabinet interiors do not match the exteriors or have the same materials or colors unless specified. If you're planning on some glass fronted cabinets in your white painted cabinet, ask if the interior is white or or wood–colored? Best advice: double–check with order department that the glass–fronted cabinets have "matching interiors".

8) **There's a reason for 15"–18" of space between the counters and the bottom of the wall cabinets.** One of my best friends demanded I mention this. Her soon–to–be–demolished kitchen has only 12" of height thanks to a poor DIY by the previous owners. "I never understood why it was so important to leave 15"–18" of space until I moved in," she says. "I hate it. The blender doesn't fit. The toaster is burning the heck out of the upper doors. It's awful! Tell them!" Okay.

9) **How will the cabinets get into the house?** Remember our gentleman from Tip #3 who was surprised his 4'×6' island came in pieces? Let's go a step further and pretend the entire island was delivered as one unit. No problem, right? Not quite. He'd need a doorway into the kitchen that was at least 36" wide. Most people say: "No problem! My front door is 36" wide!" and completely forget that the rest of the doors inside

the home are only 32" wide. Or they forget that the stairway up to the second floor kitchen doesn't have enough width to make a turn. Before you order any cabinet larger than 36" wide or high, mentally walk the delivery path into the kitchen first.

10) **Tall cabinets, such as a 96" high × 24" high cabinet, will NOT tilt upright in a 96" high room.** It's a simple law of physics — the corner of the cabinet will strike the ceiling first. The cabinet should be less. In California, ceiling and floors are rarely level (Mother Earth likes to shake us up once in awhile) so we usually make a cabinet anywhere from 4"–6" less than full ceiling height. If not, then the cabinet should be ordered with the toe kick removed. Once the cabinet's been set upright in the kitchen, it can be lifted onto a toe kick base.

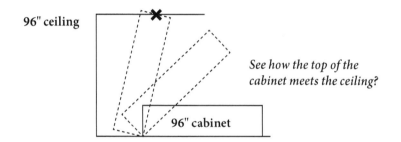

96" ceiling

See how the top of the cabinet meets the ceiling?

96" cabinet

11) **Wall cabinets deeper than 21" need support.** When I was a young designer, I learned this the hard way. A single wall cabinet 24" deep hanging on a wall is physically incapable of hanging in space without support. Add any weight to it and it'll sag at the front, which is what it did with one of my clients. (It also didn't help she was keeping a one–gallon glass jar full of pennies in it.) If the cabinet is flanked on both sides with either a wall or tall cabinets — such as an oven or pantry cabinet — that are the same depth, then the deeper wall cabinet can be screwed in and supported by the same–height tall cabinets. If they can't be supported by the tall cabinets on both sides, add the refrigerator panels.

Water: *Prevention is better than cure:* No cabinet or finish is 100% resistant against water, no matter how good they are.

Unfortunately, I've seen damage over the years that could have been prevented by knowing these two facts:

1. *Never drape a wet towel over your sink door.*
2. *Pull your coffeepots, kettles, and rice cookers out from underneath the wall cabinets when you're using them. Heated steam does twice the damage of a wet towel, and in about half the time.*

How wide do the doors swing? (Aka avoiding dings)

Before you order your cabinets, try this. Lay out the cabinets on graph paper if you haven't already done so, or perhaps you have a copy of a cabinet plan from your designer or local store.

Grab a pencil, and an architectural template which indicates door swings or arcs (you can find them at art stores and some office supply stores), and lightly draw every door open — every cabinet door, refrigerator door, and interior door into your kitchen. Also draw the dishwasher and oven/range doors open (they're approx. 21" deep.) *This will quickly show where a door:*

a) Overlaps another.
b) Hits or binds against a counter edge, a hood fan, against a dishwasher or refrigerator.
c) Only allows enough room against the wall for you to crack your knuckles against the wall if you have a grip on the handle.

If any of the above applies, then you need to tweak the design. Change some hinges, or redesign where the appliances go.

Maybe this won't solve every ding, but this small exercise will not only give you a last-minute check, but will save you from killing your friends, your kids, or your significant other every time you see that dent in your new refrigerator door. (Whoever sees the dent first is allowed to use the "not me!" defense.)

What you should know about cabinet glazes

Glazing is a stain option for cabinetry where extra stain is added on top of the first stain and then wiped off. The excess "highlights" the profiles on the door. *If you'd like it for your cabinets, there are a few helpful things to know:*

- A very ornate door will have plenty of areas for glaze to catch, but be careful if there are smooth side panels, such as refrigerator panels, — the colors between doors and panels will not be the same. It will cost more to add the door panels to these areas. If possible, view it in a showroom first. The less expensive the cabinet, the wider the color variation.
- If the doors are flat or have very little profile or design, there's not enough for the glaze to "catch" on. This is why it's not offered with smooth door styles and why you never see it on contemporary slab door styles.

Avoid old-style cleaning methods on new cabinets

Advice pops up all over the internet on how to use various soaps and cleansers to clean and touch up your cabinets. Yes, it's correct, if your cabinets weren't made in the last 20 years by a major factory. Otherwise, it's wrong.

Most factory finishes are conversion varnish finishes. The stain and finish bonds with the wood.

These cabinets should be cleaned with a mild dish soap and water only. Avoid bleaches or harsh cleansers which react badly with the finish (It turns black with bleach. Ask my 16–year–old self how I discovered this and how long the parental lecture was.)

If this seems too challenging, remember that there is help from cabinet stores to design centers to designers. If you can find someone who knows both cabinet construction and design, they'll make your life much easier.

— CHAPTER 7 —

THINKING INSIDE THE CABINET BOX
—ROLL-OUTS, PULL-OUTS
AND OTHER FITTINGS

~~Murphy's~~ Kelly's Law of pot and pan storage: The pot or pan that you need will always be stored on the bottom, at the back, and behind the rest of the pots and pans. It'll also be the last one you drag out of the cabinet.

Good kitchen storage today has at least one interior fitting to make our lives easier. For one thing, it negates Kelly's Law above, because it makes the bottom shelves both accessible and easy-to-see. Today there are many ways to access the interiors of base and pantry cabinets, but in my early design days, I needed to cajole clients into a new-fangled idea — one set of pot drawers in their new kitchens. "If you don't like them," I used to promise, "I'll give you your money back."

I'm proud (and relieved) to say I never refunded a single client once they saw how great those drawers worked (which was a good thing because I never told my parents about that little trick until years later). In this chapter, we'll address both sets of readers — those who are planning for new cabinets, and those who aren't planning for new cabinets, but would like to make their cabinets more accessible too.

The top interior fittings in order of importance:
1. *Banks of drawers*
2. *Roll–out shelves*
3. *Tray dividers for cookie sheets*
4. *Lazy Susans and Charlies*
5. *Recycle bins*
6. *Garbage bins*

What you can (and should add) to your kitchen

Banks of drawers and roll–out shelves

Without a doubt, being able to access your deepest cabinets is one of the best details you can add to your kitchen. Whether you're planning new cabinets, or keeping your existing cabinets, everyone should at least have one set of accessible base storage for pots and pans, plastic containers, or mixing bowls. Even if the budget is tight, even one set of these can make your cooking life much easier.

Here's the difference between the two:

a) Roll–out shelves are separate units hidden behind doors

b) Pull–outs are drawers

Rollout shelves are much easier to retrofit in both base cabinets and pantries, since all you're doing is adding the shelves, not replacing the doors. The pro of rollout shelves is that you can install a pair of rollout shelves in a base cabinet at any height. Or, install one on the bottom of each base cabinet if you have particularly large items, such as bulk cereal boxes, or tall stockpots, which won't fit in a standard 12"high drawer.

The con of roll–out shelves is that they're a 5–step motion: open the doors (and make sure they're open past 90–degrees or the shelf edge will scrape against the back of the door), roll out the shelf, take the item you need, push the rollout back in, close the door(s). Although, compared to a plain shelf, they're a much better option.

Pullout drawers are 3–step motion: open drawer, take item, and close drawer.

If you're not replacing your cabinets and you have an older style kitchen where the base cabinets are all cupboards with door faces and a single shelf, unless the door face is easily modified to drawers, roll-out shelves will be much easier to retrofit than rebuilding a cabinet for drawers.

Insider Definition: Retrofitting—a process of installing additional or new items to the home without affecting or altering the original design and construction.

Factory-made roll-out shelves don't always fit older existing cabinets because the cabinets weren't made to any standard. Instead, purchase the rollout shelf hardware separately, and either make the boxes yourself if you're handy, or get a handyman or carpenter to build and install them if you aren't.

Before you start, discover:

1) **What style of cabinet you have:** The frontal frame on the opening of a framed cabinet prevents us from installing side-mount hardware unless there are blocking pieces installed behind the frame that pushes the hardware to line up with the side of the opening. Otherwise the rollout shelf will be wider inside than the actual opening. You don't have this problem with frameless cabinets.

2) **Whether your cabinets have a removable center shelf:** Drawer hardware comes in two mounting styles — either on the underside of the rollout box, or on the sides. If you'd like to add a second rollout shelf in your base cabinet and the middle shelf is adjustable, it'll need to be fixed in place in order to use the bottom-mount drawer hardware.

Good hardware is costly, and worth it. The cheaper drawer hardware (also called "drawer glides") is hard to open, don't always roll properly, and last half as long. In this case, you really do get what you pay for.

Do your rollout shelves have bumpers?

Check to see if your rollout shelves have bumpers or rollers at the front corners of the shelves — this will prevent the rollout from scratching the back of the doors if someone forgets to open the doors wide.

Lazy Susans/Lazy Charlies

Both of these options are designed to provide easier access to the harder-to-reach corner cabinets. A lazy Susan is a ¾ or full circular rotating unit inside a double corner base or wall cabinet. A lazy Charlie (this could be a regional term. It's also known as a half-Susan) is a half-circle that rotates out of a blind corner. Some lazy Charlies/half-Susans might partially slide out for further access.

Do you need a lazy Susan or Charlie? That depends on you and your kitchen. They certainly make items in corners more accessible but in the design world we refer to them as secondary storage. Corner units are some of the hardest cabinets to reach into and most people will use other cabinets first. If your plan already has a lot of other base cabinets, think hard about why you need to have a Susan or Charlie. This unit might only contain Angel Food cake tins and tall glass pitchers — anything that you don't use regularly. If this is your main storage, having the rotating shelves could save your sanity.

Which corner is better?

For function, a double corner is much easier to reach into than a blind corner cabinet. (A double corner has two doors, one on each side of the corner. The doors are often hinged together and open to one side.)

If you are planning on retrofitting your kitchen, that is, adding only the interior items and not planning on replacing the actual cabinets, adding lazy Susans and lazy Charlies are almost impossible. It can be done sometimes if you're replacing the countertop because the baskets can be lowered into the cabinet. Trying to fit the baskets through the door opening won't work — you might be able to one basket sideways into the cabinet, but there won't be enough room to do two. If you can figure out a way to do it, please let me know. I haven't discovered one yet that doesn't involve installing Susans that are the ¼ of the size of the cabinet interior.

Kitchen corners — the blind corner

The blind corner is one of the cabinet areas most prone to error. Before you even get to the lazy Charlie/half–Susan inside, you need to know how it works.

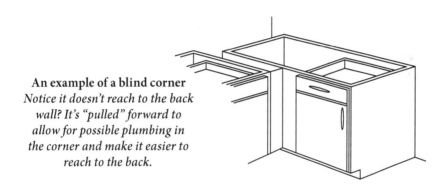

An example of a blind corner
Notice it doesn't reach to the back wall? It's "pulled" forward to allow for possible plumbing in the corner and make it easier to reach to the back.

I like to assume it's called a blind corner because you have to blindly reach with one hand and feel around for what you're looking for at the back! In reality, I believe it's because of the missing door and the blank or blind side of the cabinet.

The two top mistakes of DIY–ers and beginners are: they forget to add the filler, or they install the blind cabinet tight to the back corner.

In the previous example, the cabinet on the left is separated from the blind corner by a filler. A filler (also known as a spacer) is a stick or matching panel of wood which separates the cabinets enough so not only the adjacent drawers clear each other when opened, but the filler also can be adjusted for the depth of adjacent cabinet knobs or appliance handles.

Here's what to do. Before you install the cabinets, draw out on the floor how deep the cabinets will be, and then draw how deep the cabinet and appliance handles will be. With the advent of "pro" appliances, handles have really grown.

The filler widths in the corner are determined by the final handle depth. A dishwasher with a large architectural handle in this same design would have blocked the adjacent drawer.

A thought on self-closing drawer glides:

For those of you not familiar with soft–close drawer glides, these are a type of mechanism added to, or part of, the glides of a cabinet drawer. Some folks call them "anti–slam" buffers, for that's exactly what they do: halts the drawer front before it hits the cabinet and gently closes the rest of the way with barely a sound.

Now you might ask — why is that an option? Why isn't it standard? In some cases it is, but my mother, a Baby Boomer, doesn't like them as much as I do. She says they're hard to open for those who have grip or strength challenges. If you have difficulty opening a freezer drawer, then you might have some challenges with these. Here's how to decide if you want them.

Positive: Quiet. If you have a young family, teenagers, or a significant other who doesn't know his or her own strength — you'll love not hearing the slamslamslam! of drawers day in/day out. Probably not the best if you want to catch the dieter grabbing the cinnamon bread from the bread drawer, but excellent for that stage where the youngest likes to play "slam the drawer" again and again.

Negative: The drawers have an extra suction when you go to pull them out (especially if they're a knock–off or cheaper brand), much like a newer dishwasher or a freezer drawer. The same mechanism that sucks the drawer to the cabinet offers a bit of resistance as you start to pull, just for that first inch or so before the drawer slides out easily.

Avoid stone dust and particulates on your new drawer glides
Nothing wrecks drawer operation faster than getting stone dust in the tracks. If someone is cutting a sink hole in the granite on–site, or drilling for any holes, protect the set of drawer glides inside the cabinets.

New cabinets are easier to add options to than existing cabinets

If you're buying new factory–made cabinets, you have it easy. All you need is to decide what you want — all come pre–assembled either inside the cabinet, or ready for installation on the job site. However, if you're planning on retrofitting your existing cabinets, you'll need to check out a couple of things first.

Retrofitting existing kitchens (1980s — present)

Perhaps you have an existing kitchen that is 20–30 years old, or you live in a newer subdivision of tract homes, where most of the cabinets were factory-made. Your cabinets might be constructed as separate boxes. If that's the case, and the cabinet company or manufacturer is still around, ordering interior options might be a snap. First, you need to find the name. Is there one on a hinge or printed on a drawer? If not, do you know the builder of your subdivision, or do you have some of the original paperwork?

If none of those options is available, you might still be able to purchase some factory options from your local store or cabinet–maker if your cabinets are standard opening widths. This might take a bit of legwork or phone calls.

Pulling everything together we've just discussed, here's what you need to know before you start the search:

1) **Is the cabinet frame or frameless?** Good thing we covered how to discover this in Chapter 6. With frame cabinets, the frame makes the openings smaller than the interior. With frameless cabinets, the opening is the same as the box size — there is no frontal frame. Either way affects how hardware — whether for roll–out shelves or pull–out garbage bins — will be installed.

2) **Are the cabinets made as separate boxes and each set of drawers and doors clearly separate from the next cabinet?** (Another way to tell for framed cabinets — there is usually a vertical seam between each cabinet where the individual boxes were joined together.)

3) **If it's not a box, what is it?** Some frame cabinets are still constructed today with entire sections of cabinets built together as one big cabinet; the shelves run the entire length behind the doors. This is called a unitized system. These systems may be factory–made or in–house. Today's interior fittings require cabinet sides, or at least some sort of interior separation or blocking.

4) **Is your home high–end with custom cabinets?** High–end custom frame cabinets which are factory–or custom–produced, can be built both as a box system and unitized. In other words, the boxes can be built as an entire section and you won't see the seam between the cabinets. Yet, when you open the door, you'll see the sides and back of a typical box cabinet. Most high–end cabinets have their name stamped somewhere on the cabinet — perhaps a drawer box or on a hinge. If you find a name, do a search online to see if you can find the company, and order from them.

Even with items b) and d), there are still multiple quirks and design aspects which change with each line.

I've worked with over 12–14 different cabinet lines in my lifetime, and every one of them has something different from the others — whether it's a way of installation or a different style bracket. There's absolutely no guarantee that Brand A's interior fittings will fit into Brand B's cabinets, even if the cabinets look the same (although you might have better luck with stock cabinets). This is how the manufacturers ensure that you stay with their brand.

Retrofitting existing kitchens (1880s — 1970s)

For those of you who have existing older cabinets that may have been made in-house, there wasn't a standardized system. You may have the oldest style of unitized cabinets — where the frontal frame and the counters are the only pieces holding the shelves together, without any cabinet backs or sides. Once you remove the counter, they fall apart. One way to tell is to check for a back to the cabinets — if there isn't one, it's the older style. Also check to see if the cabinets were nailed to the wall or screwed. The older style used nails.

You definitely have to be careful if you're not replacing the cabinets — take out one section and the entire piece could fall apart.

For you, you're going to need some good DIY experience, or a cabinet-maker, or a carpenter to retrofit what you want. Your options will have to be built onsite, and not all options will be available to you.

Areas where people think items should fit (and they don't):
1. Full-size garbage/recycle bins under the sink: We can't — the plumbing drains get in the way. You might be able to install a roll-out shelf in the sink base, or mount a small door-mounted unit.

2. Installing tray dividers in wall cabinets. Again, no. Well, let me take that back. You can, but you'll only be able to store small cookie sheets or cooling racks—the interior of a wall cabinet is 11" deep at most (unless specified deeper). I rarely recommend providing dividers above your head, esp. if we're storing heavy marble baking blocks or bulky butcher blocks.

Clear as glass:

Glass doors have always been a popular choice that have never really come and gone like most trends. Over the years, we've seen glass range from the original poured glass with the bubbles still showing (think "antique" or "water" glass) to clear glass to textured (think "reed" or the lined glass of the 1940s) to today — where it's all over the place depending on regional preferences.

Some cabinet companies supply various styles of glass, and some don't. While you can get clear, obscure, or textured glass directly from them, you don't have to order the glass from the cabinet company. Visit a stained glass shop in your town (if you have one). Some of the types of glass with colors or swirls can be beautiful.

Think about your shelves inside your glass-fronted cabinets

While a lot of people give serious consideration to the types and styles of glass for the door, many don't think about the shelves. This can be disappointing for someone who wants the entire focus to be on the glass and not what is behind it.

Whether the shelves are wood or painted, if your door glass is clear or only partially obscure, the shelves will become a strong line element to the look — unless you consider adding glass shelves.

Here's a note: glass shelves cost extra, and, no, you don't get a credit for the existing wood shelves that come with a stock factory cabinet. (In the case of most stock cabinets, the boxes are made and stored in advance, and pulled off the shelves for your order. It's more trouble for them to remove and store the shelves somewhere and then figure out which size shelves go with which new cabinet. For custom cabinets, the cabinets are made when you order them, so there are no extra shelves.)

An example of the prairie–style mullions with glass shelves.The design would have been lost if the shelves had been matching wood.

If you're planning on adding some mullions to your glass doors, which are strips of wood applied in a grid pattern as part of the door, then you really need to consider glass for the interior shelving. We add the mullions for a bit of design detail, and there's nothing worse than when your elegant Prairie style mullion doors (shown here) are crossed with multiple other lines that weren't part of the design.

There are two solutions:

a) Glass shelves on the interior.
b) Frosted or obscure glass on the door.

Think safety

Having glass on a wall cabinet isn't usually a concern — the cabinets are out of the way of elbows and knees. However, if you plan on having glass doors in the lower section of a pantry or a base cabinet — consider specifying tempered glass for your doors and shelves. Not all glass, especially textured, will come in a tempered glass, and your cabinet company might not be able to get it.

Insider Definition: Tempered glass is glass produced with either thermal or chemical processes to be stronger than regular glass. If the glass is hit hard enough, it breaks into chips instead of shards.

If they don't, look to a glass company, or a glass shower door company or anyone who specializes in home glass applications near you. Let them know the exact size needed and they'll give you a price. Don't forget to ask if that includes installation. In most cases, it's a simple case of using silicon bead or a nail–in trim to install the glass, but if you're not handy, having someone else perform the work might save some aggravation.

Where to get glass shelves (when you're not buying new cabinets)

If you're not buying new cabinets, where can you get glass shelves? The same companies above. (Also check custom mirror companies — they might have a glass shop as well.) With glass shelves, the wider and deeper the cabinet, the thicker the glass shelf should be to support the weight.

So here's the rule I grew up with:
a) ¼" thickness minimum for any 12" deep cabinet up to 27" wide
b) ⅜" for anything 30"–36".
c) Anything larger than 36" wide should be approached with caution — or, at least, extra bracing. Most glass shelving is supported on the cabinet sides. You might require an extra support or bracket to safely hold up the middle.

3 tips for glass shelves

1) The thicker the glass, the greener the edge. In a cabinet with a wood interior, you might not even notice. But in a white cabinet, you will. There are other glass colors that vary from clear to light blue, but they're not standard. Ask your glass supplier if they have other options.
2) If you're buying the glass separately, be aware that the edges come square unless specified "polished" one long (which means one of the long sides, usually the front edge, will be polished). The next step up is a pencil edge polish — it looks like a soft D if you look at it sideways.
3) Avoid bevels on your glass shelves — you won't see them, and the front angle on the edge provide a nice tipping point for glasses or mugs; the last thing you want.

Planning on textured glass? The majority of the fingerprints, stains, and spots happen on the outside of the cabinet. Textured glass has one rough side and one smooth side. Make your life easier—Install the smooth side of the glass on the exterior.

A final tip: Not all companies line up the shelves with the mullions

In the higher end cabinets they do, but if you're planning on stock cabinets, check to see if the holes line up. There is nothing as annoying (if you notice these things) than to order a nice mullion door and having the shelf sit just below or just above where the mullion is. It's not as noticeable with glass shelves, but is very noticeable with wood shelves.

Where specialty fittings and glass were once the territory of higher-end homes, they're now available for all.

If a new kitchen is out of the picture for now, at least consider making it accessible (glass may or may not be in the picture). Save yourself from ever crawling into a cupboard again.

CHAPTER 8

GETTING A GRIP ON KNOBS, HANDLES, AND HINGES

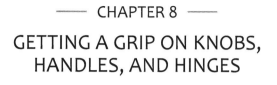

There are hidden aspects to installing cabinetry hardware, hinges, and other hardware that need to be thought through regarding size, placement, and design. This chapter will discuss common mistakes, such as a handle damaging a side wall (or a knuckle) due to insufficient space between the handle and wall, as well as what a designer looks for in cabinetry hardware.

You would think that it's easy to add cabinet knobs and pulls, wouldn't you? I used to think so too, until 4 million different styles, colors, and quantities hit the market.

Insider Definition: Cabinet hardware — another name for cabinet knobs and pulls.

If you think a knob is simply a knob and you can save money in this area, let me demonstrate how I learned the hard way. When I was a baby designer, I figured I could save money on my handles. Why spend $6.00, $8.00, or even $10.00 dollars a knob? That was a fortune! Nope, I found a handle that was $1.29.

I was so smug, right until 10 months later, when all the finish wore off and I had to buy them a second time.

By the time I clued in, I paid in total about $6.50 per drawer front, and I still had crappy quality. If I'd bought the good ones in the beginning, I would have saved myself a lot of time and aggravation. It's painful to have a designer mother who practically radiates "I told you so."

Life's too short. Your handles are the most, er, handled item (with the exception of the refrigerator and counters) in your kitchen. Pay for a decent quality. The best advice I can offer is never just look at a handle and buy it without testing first.

Here's how I look for a good handle or knob:

a) Feel the weight — they should have a decent heft. Lesser priced (and lesser quality) handles are made with a hollow cast or a cheaper metal which can feel very lightweight.
b) Check two or three side–by–side — is the color and the finish even on all of them?
c) Buy one and feel the backs and edges — poor quality knobs may have sharp points or edges that can cut.
d) Do they have any hooks or catches which can pinch a finger?

Buy a couple — take them home. Place them on the cabinet door and drawer (if you have a sample). See if you can grab them. If your fingers can't fit in the space between the underside of the handle and the cabinet, you've got a problem. Better to find out in advance than to install them all and find out later.

Be careful of knobs of a certain shape, i.e. box handles, or triangular, or any type that needs to be set in a certain way. They never stay that way; they twist in everyday use, so if you're a precisionist like me, you're compelled to straighten every single knob when you walk into the room.

Round knobs aren't a problem; if they twist, you certainly don't see it, unless they have a certain pattern, say grapes or leaves which look better in an upright position.

Some companies have thought the product through and added one or two small bumps on the back side or mounting plate of the handle; thus, when the knob is screwed into the drawer/door, the bumps dig into the drawer front, locking the knob into place. Or some knobs have two screws instead of one.

Which is better, knob or pull?

This is a loaded question, answerable only by you and really depends on the size of the handle or knob and the size of your hands, as well as the hands of the people who will be opening the doors and drawers.

There's also the aspect of arthritis or problems gripping with hands, or pain in the wrists that need to be considered. For this case, handles are typically easier to grasp or latch onto.

It's really all about the grip: sizing the width and depth of your hardware and purchasing a couple in advance before you buy the entire lot can really be an eye opening experience.

What we want is the base of a handle or knob, which is called the shank, to be long enough for our fingers to comfortably close around them.

A stubby or short-shank knob on a recessed drawer front will be almost impossible to open because half the grip of the shank is lost in the recess.

Top drawers of a base cabinet are typically the narrowest. The knob in this section doesn't leave much grasping room for larger fingers.

Now we've lost part of the handle inside that narrow recess. Not to mention that the inner profile of the cabinet door will be scratched by longer nails.

If your cabinets are frameless, there might be a third option — channels or separations between the doors and drawers which are curved in a backwards "C" or "D" profile, so that you can grab the door without needing pulls. It's a "new-old" trick, in that I was designing with it for years in the 1980s, and then it went away when all the fancy new cabinet hardware appeared. Not all cabinet lines have this option, and not all designers out there even know what it is. But if you ask if there is a frameless channel option, and the designer brightens up, you've found your person.

Here's a tip: this style can be rough on both the channel and your lovely, long fingernails (if you have them), as your fingernails will either gouge the channel or will cause you to chip a nail.

Insider Definition: Breakaway Screws: Some cabinet hardware comes with screws that are not long enough to fit through a drawer box and a drawer front. Breakaway screws are longer screws that can be cut to fit the length you need. They come in 4mm and ⁸⁄₃₂" which affects how the screw winds into the hardware — check to see if it'll work before buying or simply purchase screws that are 1¾" long.

Examples of a breakaway screw (top) and a regular hardware screw (bottom)

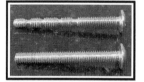

Can I mix and match different sizes and shapes?

Absolutely. Scaling the handle size to the cabinet size is done all the time — simply because a cabinet drawer may be too narrow to fit an elongated handle, or perhaps it's the opposite — a drawer may be almost 36" wide and require something more substantial than a knob or a 3" long handle.

However be careful of using too many sizes because too much variation can become a distraction. And one of the challenges that we all forget is that while the handles will look great on one cabinet, having different sizes side–by–side along the same wall can distract the eyes in a way we don't really want.

I always draw elevations for this reason — to see how the handles balance beside one another. (Imagine a pantry with large handles next to a small bank of drawers with small handles next to a large drawer with medium handles.) The most sizes I've ever used have been 4 — and the 4th were the large–scale appliance handles, but there's always a future kitchen that will break my guidelines. A larger–scale kitchen "gets away" with more than a small kitchen does.

If you're truly stuck, study kitchen photos online or look in your favorite magazines.

Some of my handle combinations have been:

- knobs on all the upper cabinets, handles on the base cabinets.
- knobs on the top drawers with handles on the bases (handles or knobs on the top cabinets).
- handles everywhere with a smaller scale version only where the larger won't fit.
- all the same handles with something fun and unique on the glass door cabinets.

There is something fun and fresh about adding one or two pieces of hardware that are truly beautiful or works of art or simply amusing — especially knobs because they're so easy to change if you really wanted to. With all the great handles and knob choices available, why not add a piece or two just because you can?

There's always a catch: the 6 places hardware snags your design

1) Remember our lazy Charlie? If you put a handle on the door and drawer of a lazy Charlie that is adjacent to a drawer on the opposite cabinet, the door/drawer opposite will not open. Well, it will — only until it hits the handle.

2) Rule number 1 applies if you're installing banks of drawers or base cabinets in both corners instead of a lazy susan. Give the handles room to move!

3) Beware of handles with sharp ends that can catch on clothes. Some decorative handles are lovely, but they're hard on pant pockets!

4) Test the installation of a door handle next to a bumped–out cabinet. Is there enough room between the cabinet and your grasp or do your fingers (or fingernails) scrape the side of the protruding cabinet when you grab the handle?

5) Do your knobs have a specific design other than circle? All knobs loosen at some point on the screw. You don't notice on a circle, but you do on any other shape. I once specified a pair of knobs shaped like martini glasses, which we joked that one could tell it was 5p.m. by the way the glass was tilted by the end of the day. If this will drive you crazy, avoid all oval, diamond, bar-shaped, or specialty knobs (unless you check the tip in the following box), or install them on lesser-used cabinets.

6) Avoid wall divots: A common mistake in handle design is not thinking through what happens when installing a straight cabinet in a corner and tight to a side wall. Hinges at 110-degrees open wider than the side wall at 90-degrees, so either your cabinet knob or your fist will hit the wall first. Do yourself a favor. Leave some space between the wall and the cabinet. Install a 3" cabinet filler between them. Or, if you can't do that, at least invest in a door stop or a wall bumper.

Locking your handle in place:
Check the back of your potential cabinet knobs for a pair of small bumps, like the two you see on either side of the screw hole. These small bumps indent into the cabinet door or drawer, and prevent the knob from turning or twisting.

How to size your handles correctly for your drawers

I wish there was a hard-and-fast rule, but there isn't. Here are my rules of thumb:

Before you buy, check the width of both your smallest and widest drawers. Buy a few sizes and see what looks best.

If the cabinet is larger than 27" wide and the handles are 4" or less, I sometimes recommend using 2 handles, spaced 3"–5" from each side of the drawer.

Installing handles and knobs on doors

Installing hardware isn't tough — it's about making sure that all of them are installed evenly. If you're planning on installing handles yourself, here's a way to do it.

Cut a piece of plywood — any size will do. For the doors, place it in the corner of the door where the handle will be. (It helps if you're a beginner to remove the doors and set them on a flat surface. It also helps if the plywood piece is absolutely square so you can line it up with a door corner.)

Mark the placement of the shanks where the screws will be installed on the plywood and when you've set the exact placement, drill the holes through both the door and plywood (take care you don't drill through onto your surface!).

Now you have a template that can be applied to the rest of the doors, and you'll always have the exact measurement every time.

What you need to know about hinges

Both framed and frameless cabinets have had hidden hinges for years, but it wasn't always so. Mid-century cabinets once had hinges that showed on the exterior of the cabinet — called a knife hinge. Older traditional homes used the beauty of inset hinges with elaborate finials which are still used on many inset door styles today. The beauty of these hinges is that they enabled a door to swing fully open almost 180-degrees; the challenge was that they made it almost impossible to adjust a door as the home settled.

Insider Definition — Inset Hinges: Inset doors (where the frame and the door are flush) use an inset hinge. This style of cabinet must be installed perfectly, or the doors will scrape on the frame when they're opened. The inset hinges don't allow for a lot of adjustment, something for those of you living in earthquake areas to think about.

The new hidden hinges have 6–way adjustment — back and forth, side-to-side, and up–and–down. The standard hinges that most cabinetry has only opens 90-to 110-degrees, but here's what we in the industry are aware of that you may not be: 170–degree hinges are available. They're a bit bulky, but they can be a real boon to your design when you need them.

An example of 110–degree hinge on a frameless style cabinet.

If you're planning on replacing your hinges, make sure the person who plans to do the work either installs the new hardware in a slightly different location than the existing holes, or plans on adding new strips of wood (or "blocking") for the hinges to be installed into. This takes a bit more labor and obviously costs more, but there's a reason for it. The hinge screw holes take a lot of abuse over the years, and with enough wear, the screws may "strip" the original drill hole. Pull too hard on your door and it could fall off the cabinet. Not all holes are stripped, but better to check first.

Baby–or earthquake–proofing (Surprisingly, not the same thing.)

Ahh, the baby years...where all cabinets with cleaners and alcohol need to be safe from little hands. If you have handles, most people use elastics or string to tie the handles together, but that's not always the best solution. What do you do if you don't have any handles on your cabinets?

If you'd like to have locks on your doors, you need to know first what style your cabinets are. Are they frameless or framed? Do you want the lock to show or be hidden?

For framed cabinets, there's a catch that can be applied to the back of the door which hooks onto the frame. It's a bit annoying because it's a two-step process: open the door an inch to expose the catch, and then press on it to release the hook before finally opening the door, but it does work really well for those first couple of years.

For frameless cabinets, this option isn't possible — there's no frame for the hook to catch on. Fortunately, there's a two-part magnetic catch that works well for frameless cabinets — once the door closes, the catch locks into place inside the cabinet, and can only be opened by applying a magnet opener to the surface of the door.

Most of these locks come with two magnets, just in case one magnet is left inside the cabinet or drawer. (Guilty.)

For your online searches, look for "child-proof cabinet latches" for the framed cabinets, and "magnetic locks for cabinets for the frameless cabinets."

CHAPTER 9

HEADS–UP ON COUNTERS

Each type of countertop — laminate, tile, solid surface, quartz, granite, glass, cement, and stainless steel — has its own sets of pros and cons depending on its properties. This chapter will discuss not only those properties, but the main focus will be on counter edges and overhangs, as well as stone and quartz counters as they have the most costly mistakes.

Counter depths have also changed over the years, along with thicknesses, edge details, and other design considerations.

15 ways to leave your counter: the pros and cons

Behind every person who has ever said, "I hate my (fill in the blank) counter", is a person who picked a counter for the wrong reasons — whether it was because they fell in love with the looks without asking about the function, or everyone else had it. Counters should be selected for function first, and ultimately how they can live up to your family's lifestyle and habits.

I've listed below all the functional pros and cons of the counters as relayed by my clients over the years. These are listed in order of pricing, but it's a bit nebulous at the top end, as the edge details and finishing touches tend to hopscotch the price with each addition.

Counter material	Pros:	Cons:	Something to think about:
Laminate (Wilson-Art, Formica)	• Cost. • Can look great—new photo finishes are better than ever.	• Will scratch if cut on Can't put hot items directly on counter.	• Strong abrasives can remove the top plastic layer. Once that happens, you've reached the paper substrate, which leads to staining. • If you're building a home and the budget's tight, consider laminate.
Wood	• Cost. • Great for cutting on, but will show abuse.	• Easily stained.	• Oil with food–friendly oil according to manuf. or wood–worker's instructions. • Surface grain rises and needs to be scraped. • Depending on the report, surprisingly good at removing bacteria away from the surface of the wood.
Solid Surfaces (Corian, Avonite)	• Seamless look. • Can integrate sinks.	• Shows scratches.	• Best thing about solid surfaces: you can abuse the heck out of them, and then call the fabricator to refinish the top when needed.
Tile	• The very best for placing hot pots on—the heat flashes to the grout and dissipates. • The squarer the edge of the tile, the tighter the grout joint.	• Wide grout lines are hard to bake on— unless you like your cookies with lines in them...	• Some tiles, such as porcelain tiles, hold up better than some ceramics. • If individual tiles crack, they can be removed and replaced. Make sure to order a few spares.

Counter material	Pros:	Cons:	Something to think about:
Granites	• Can take heat (caveat at far right). • Can be fabricated with matt or other textured finishes.	• Cutting on the surface dulls knives and in some cases, can scratch the granite.	• Some granite has fissures, quartz inclusions (pockets of clear or white crystals) which can sometimes be a weak structural point in granite. Put something too hot or too cold on this area, and the slab could crack. • Can absorb water, which eventually dries, but a bit of a shock if your sink area is wet and your counter is darker there than anywhere else.
Marbles/ Lime-stone	• Smooth, cool surface, perfect for baking and rolling dough. • Can come in matt or other finishes.	• Can be etched and may stain. • Depending on mineral content, susceptible to acidic foods and hard water.	• If your colors are light and bright, light–colored marbles and limestones are a good color choice vs. darker–colored granites.
Glass Counters	• Beautiful.	• Hard, loud surface, glossy.	• Lots of windows will highlight streaks on counters.
Quartz Counters	• Engineered for strength, no worries about fissures. • Non–absorbent.	• Same as glass with the hard, loud surface.	• Shouldn't place extremely hot pots on the counter.

Counter material	Pros:	Cons:	Something to think about:
Stainless steel	• Non–porous can take abuse.	• Can also dent and scratch.	• Counter of choice for chefs and caterers.
Zinc and copper	• Beautiful surface that develops patinas and wear quickly.	• If you don't like scratches, you won't like these two.	• Copper has some antibacterial properties.
Recycled Paper	• Bonus for recycling content. • Quiet surface.	• Does absorb and stain.	• Surprisingly more durable than you might think, but don't treat it like a granite.
Soap-stone	• Durable, marks do come out.	• Tough on your good knives.	• If not oiled, ends up looking like there's a soap film on the surface. Takes a lot of oil at the beginning.

If you find yourself arguing any of them, keep in mind this is just one opinion. I've seen a marble counter pristine after a decade and another which was stained and pitted. Both clients were perfectly happy with the choice. The caveat is that you need to understand the properties of the counter thoroughly before you buy.

There are two reasons for not selecting the counter best suited for you:

a) **Neighborhood perceived value:** If you don't want to hurt your chances on re–sale within 6 months to 5 years, but your counter is falling apart, you'll need to stick to what the neighborhood has. If the rest of your neighbors are installing laminate, and you install custom slab granite, you won't get the value out of it (although you might sell faster, unless you're in an area that hates granite.) Conversely, if everyone has custom slab granite and you install laminate counters, you're not keeping up with the perceived value and it will hurt you when you sell.

b) **Desire:** You know your busy family. They leave coffee rings on the counter, and you need something that will at least hide the toast crumbs. But you've had your heart set on wood counters ever since you saw them, and they make your heart beat faster. You know you're going to have more maintenance and staining. You also know wood is not too difficult to repair. In this case, you know what to expect, and you still want them.

Nothing wrong with that, as long as everyone is prepared.

To Trivet or Not to Trivet?

What's a trivet? A trivet can be a pot holder or a square of ceramic tile or a wood block or any other material that we place hot items on instead of directly onto the counters.

"But why?" you may ask. "That's why I'm buying Brand X material so I don't need to use a trivet."

I grew up with expert stone people who cautioned me to always use a trivet. Here's what they told me: "Stone is affected by fast extremes of hot and cold. You never know what small fissures may be hiding in your stone until you slap a boiling pot of potatoes on the counter. It might crack. It might not. It all depends on the stone but we still use trivets for extremes."

Manufacturers of solid surfaces and quartz counters also recommend using a trivet for hot items, including electric fryers, crock pots and any on-the-counter small appliance which can overheat the counter surface. It's not that the counters are in danger of cracking, it's because there's a danger of burning the resins that bind these products together.

Even with laminate tops, I'd suggest avoiding using these small appliances over a seam. Over the years I've seen some electric fryers get hot enough on the bottom for the heat to melt the glue holding the laminate to the substrate material underneath.

What if you only want to replace your counter?

Although many people have no problem replacing counters (indeed, most DIY and real estate websites make it sound as it's as easy as snapping your fingers), it's may not be a cost-effective and worthwhile endeavor.

Before you start, let's do away with the misconceptions:

It's easy to remove the existing countertop.

Not always. As mentioned in the previous chapter, pre–1980s cabinets were built in the home, not in a factory. There were no standards. Some were simply frames to hold the doors in place. There were no backs to them (you see the wall when you open the doors), and the shelves ran the entire length of all the cabinets. The counters acted as part of the cabinet construction.

This is a long–winded way of saying remove the countertop and the cabinets may fall apart. Can someone rebuild the cabinets to stay together and still replace the counter? Of course. It takes a bit more skill than enthusiasm, so if this is your first DIY project and you have no woodworking skills, this might not be the project to start with.

I can replace the counters now and re–use them later when I'm ready to do the cabinets.

Heavy counters, such as stones and quartz, can rarely be transferred (and in most cases, may break because they were fastened well). U–shaped kitchens are the worst case scenario as counter seams don't come apart easily and it's difficult to support all points when lifting it off the existing cabinets, especially if it's ½ ton of granite! The counters are prone to weakness at a cutout area and any dip or twist in the moving could cause these weaker areas to snap.

My cabinets are fine — I'm good, right?

Yes, but I'd keep a close eye on the remaining lifespan of your appliances and plumbing fixtures. Many cook tops and ranges have specific cutout requirements and notches. Even if you decide to replace the cabinets later and can transfer your new granite counter, it could be for nothing if the new appliances won't fit.

If the kitchen was built or remodeled within the last decade.

The cabinets are fairly decent, and you like the layout, but still can't stand the counters, you have the best option of all. Have fun. Remember to select your appliances carefully so they'll fit with your existing cabinets.

If someone visits our showroom with the intention of adding granite or any stone or quartz counters to their existing 1960s cabinets, I recommend against it if the cabinets will be replaced in the foreseeable future. Older cabinets were shallower than today's kitchens, and won't transfer to fit the newer, deeper cabinets.

However, nothing is absolute. You might find a cabinet maker who could custom make your new cabinets to match the granite depth. Or you could find that removing the granite and transferring it to the new cabinets is easier with the following:

- **Simple layouts, small kitchens, and some island tops.** Galley shapes or single pieces counters, such as island tops, can sometimes be transferred. This is easiest if it's laminate. Also easier with a newer style (1980s or later) cabinet, so at least you know the depths will be the same should you decide to replace the cabinets later.

- **The counter is a solid surface.** If a piece does break, there's a fair chance it can be cut away and a new piece installed. Once it's seamed together, you won't be able to tell.

Where to cut back if budget is tight

Counter edges

Here's where the hidden costs are — the fancier the edge, the more expensive it is (except for wood — as long as the person routing the edge has the right bit). If my clients are watching their budget , this is one of the areas I look to for cutting back — selecting a standard or less expensive edge can sometimes save anywhere from $300.00–$3,000.00 depending on the kitchen and layout.

Edge detail at a sink

Anytime a sink is mounted under the counter, it costs more than simply "dropping" in a sink (the ones with an edge or flange). That edge (usually with marbles, granites, and quartz products) has to be polished or finished, which is where your extra cost comes in.

Pay attention to what the perceived value of the counter is in your area. For example, it's considered a part of higher end design for counter edges to be either a 1¼" or 1½" thick edge. Yet I have seen in magazines and in show homes, that this edge is eliminated in favor of a straight ¾" edge, like so:

An example of a ¾" thick (2 cm) counter.

Why? It's cheaper, and gives the homebuyer the bragging rights of having granite. But it would be perceived as a cost–cutting shortcut in some neighborhoods and not up to par with the value of the home.

I have no objection to either method, although after working with the thicker edge for so many years, I find the thinner one lacks visual weight. Does it affect the counter efficiency? No. But here's the interesting part: when you're dealing with our beloved perceived value, there's no use fighting it, especially if this isn't your forever home.

A thought for the Reluctant Remodeler
Planning an entire kitchen, but the budget needs to get the kids through college too? While we'd all like to do everything at once, sometimes is just isn't possible.

Consider a laminate counter, and hold off on the fancy backsplash for now. Pre–formed laminate tops are a fraction of stone price.

By the time the kids graduate, the budget might be there to replace the laminate with the counter and backsplash you want.

The wonder of personal taste is that it's forever changing — the latest trend from Europe the past year is ultra thin counters, so who knows where we'll be in a few years time?

There are a lot of different style counter edges out there — generally the thicker the edge or more detail it is, the more it costs, so the Europeans might be onto something.

An example of a stepped counter — not my favorite for bakers.

A square edge may be inexpensive, but the edge is the most fragile point of any piece. If you're like me, and tend to drop pots and other items on the counter in your haste, know that a square corner doesn't hold up well to abuse. Consider instead a slight eased edge, or a bevel at the corner or even a more pronounced radius edge at the top.

Also think about how the fancier stepped counter edges (like above) will hold up. Will it bother you to clean flour off this edge? Will you end up putting glasses or mugs at the (tipping) edge of the counter? The first is not really a huge factor as a quick wipe is easy to do; the second is more serious.

Bull nose Edge: A bull nose counter edge (which is technically not a bull nose, but a half circle) is a perfect channel for water to follow from the top of the counter to the underside and into the drawer. Something to consider if your family isn't careful with water clean up.

A final detail — If you're doing this yourself, watch that the counter edge doesn't hang down over the front of the drawers and doors. Older style cabinets were built with more space between the drawers and the underside of the counter than they are today.

How to tell when an old tile counter has been replaced: *when an extra horizontal piece of cabinet trim is added between the top of the cabinet doors and the counter. It fills in the gap left by the old counter and the thinner new counter.*

Hanging 10: When is support needed for your counter overhangs?

We always get conflicted reports of on how far a counter can extend beyond the cabinets without support partly because it always depends on the heaviness of the materials, the length of the proposed overhang, and the existing support.

If extra seating area at the island or peninsula is your dream, but you don't want to add any extra legs or brackets, you need to know what the maximum depths the counter can *overhang*.

Lighter counters can always extend farther than heavier counters. For example, laminate or wood counters can extend up to 12"–14" deep. For the heavier materials, such as stone or quartz, 10"–12" is a recommended depth of extension before we require additional support. *The final design decisions rest on the following factors:*

a) Thickness of the material: Some fabricators install steel supports underneath the granite (or in the sub–ply if they're installing ¾" granite). The challenge is the corners of the overhangs, which can be vulnerable to someone hefting a hip to sit on the edge (I can't reach that high.)

b) A bar bracket will offer some support but the really best support for deeper counters are brackets which carry the weight of the front edge down to the floor. If you plan on deeper depths, then a leg or floor–to–counter bracket offers some of the best support.

The easy secret for choosing the right bar stool height

I usually refer to the seating at counters as bar stools, although I'm aware that they're also called counter stools in other parts of the country.

Whatever you call them, stools usually come in three standard heights. (Be aware that some bar stool manufacturers list the entire height of the stool from floor to top of the backrest. You're looking for seat height from floor to top of cushion.)

a) 17–19" high (standard chair height is 18" high)

b) 24"–26" high (counter height)

c) 30"–32" high (bar height)

Use a simple trick to determine what stool height you need: Subtract 12" from your counter height. That's it.

Thus, a 36" kitchen counter requires a 24" counter stool; a raised 42" bar requires a 30"high stool. Note where the arm heights are and how they interact with the countertop when the stools are pushed in.

Wall Cabinets to Counter — Repeat tip: Wall cabinets that extend down to the counter can't be installed until after the countertop is installed — something the cabinet maker or installer should know because it will take two separate trips to finish the job.

Polished vs. honed stone counters

If you're planning on polished counters, lighting will become important, especially if we're talking polished stone counters. If there are no windows or poor lighting, the granite which sparkled so invitingly in the sunlight at the slab yard looks lifeless in a kitchen or bath. It needs good lighting to "pop" the crystals in the slab, especially if the color is dark.

Or, as one of my clients laughingly says, "I like the flecks in my granite, but my mother thinks the flecks look like bread crumbs when the lights aren't on. They drive her crazy every time she visits."

If you have plenty of windows or strong lighting, darker, glossy counters act as a mirror. They reflect the light from the window, and how the lights are positioned under your wall cabinets. Bright lighting is like the sun on water; it reflects everything.

As a contrast, you won't have those issues with honed stones. However, they do show oils — cooking oils, oils from hands, smears, and some scratches.

So, bring a couple of samples home, if possible. View it by daylight and night. Place it next to a window and eat toast on it. Smear it with a cloth and see how easy it is to clean up.

That way your expectations and the reality match *before* the stone goes in. And your granite can look like you meant it to.

This also applies to any counter that you're dreaming of. Some manufacturers offer online ordering of their samples and I encourage you to check them out. That small pre–purchase and testing of your counter choice might be the best money you ever spent.

CHAPTER 10

WE'VE GOT YOUR BACK (SPLASH)

It's no secret that backsplashes are one of the more important decorative elements of today's kitchens. Whether the backsplash material is tile or stone or stainless steel or even wood, there are a myriad of design details that must be considered in order to achieve the look you want.

What's not stressed enough in design books or magazines:

- How much outlets and switches, light rail, lighting and trim are affected by the backsplash material and vice–versa.
- How badly crooked walls affect today's complex tile designs.
- How much one needs to understand the installation properties of a product. For example, an un–grouted glass tile in the store can appear radically different grouted.

The way I look at backsplashes has nothing to do with color or texture, and more to do with thickness, size, installation methods, and cleaning properties. In this chapter, I'll help you with why we should look for those details, and what to watch for as you create your personal style.

Backsplash thicknesses — granite, tile, glass, and more

One of the biggest mistakes a beginner makes is assuming that all backsplashes are the same thickness, and they're not.

If your backsplash is thicker than a standard ⅜" thick tile — say a custom tile with a thickset installation (see definition on next page), then this is something that your electrician needs to know; otherwise, it'll be tough installing the switch plates for outlets because the boxes will be set too far back. This is a complete pain after the tile is installed. It takes far more fiddling after the tile is installed to use longer screws, add a box extender, or, in some cases, remove and re-install the boxes so they sit flush with the tile. It may also result in some tile breakage, which can further delay the project.

Save yourself the time and aggravation — let the electrician know so that he or she can install adjustable boxes and enough wire, and the rest of the installation can run from there.

A quick note: you can't leave flammable materials exposed to the electrical box. If you're planning on a nice thick wood wainscot as a backsplash and the electrical boxes are recessed, the boxes must fit the inside depth from front to back to prevent any electrical problems from burning the wood. Using longer screws to bridge the gap between the wood thickness and a recessed standard electrical box won't pass code. The boxes will require box extenders (found at an electrical supply store or your local hardware store). That way the wood is protected.

Insider Definition: *Thin-set vs. Thick-set tile installation*
Both of these refer to tile installation methods and the thickness of the mortar bed behind the tile.

With thick–set (also called mud–set), the tile-setter builds a water-proof and steel reinforced backing, before applying a thick level of mortar, or mud. The tile is then applied to this. The overall thickness is 1".

With thin–set, the tile is adhered directly onto a backer board using a much thinner layer of mortar. The overall thickness with a standard tile is ½".

Of the two, the thick–set is the older method and more labor-intensive; many areas use the newer thin–set. I've seen both and prefer the thin–set because I can use thinner borders.

I might ask for thick–set if I'm working in an older character
home where the thick–set is in period.

Partial–height backsplashes

First, let's consider what a backsplash is for — to protect your walls from
water, and other moisture, whether it's orange juice spills or pancake batter.
This is most important at the junction where the countertop and the wall
meet. The rest of the wall, or backsplash, from the counter to the underside
of the wall cabinets, is the area most subjected to splashing of liquids during
cooking or mixing.

For years, the most reasonable way to trim the budget was to select a
countertop with an integrated 3"–4" splash. There was no seam between
counter and backsplash, which meant no issues from water damage; however,
one of the challenges was that it was straight. If your walls were extremely
uneven, there was no way of hiding the gap between the backsplash and
the waviness of the walls.

As time went on, this backsplash morphed into a stronger design
element — a separate band of material in the form of laminate, wood, or a
single row of tile.

A single row of backsplash with the full splash only behind the range top.

In some ways, this design was — and still is — the fastest and easiest to install. There is no need to consider the exact placement of electrical switches and outlets (other than to make sure they're above the backsplash, which most outlets are.) I've designed some very beautiful tile elements using a single row of tile and a bull-nosed tile edge. It's a sensible way to cut back on the budget and allows some flexibility to add paint colors in this space.

Full-height backsplashes

When someone asks whether you're going to have a full-height back splash, they're really asking if you're planning on having tile installed on the wall between the counter and the underside of the cabinets. For most standard kitchens, this means an 18" high backsplash in most areas, with a 30"–36" space behind the range or cook top. *With this type of design, the items to be concerned with are:*

a) The outlet and switch placements — will they affect any design details?

b) How the exposed edges of the backsplash material will be finished.

c) How the windows and trims will affect the backsplash — will a tile be installed to the edges of a window, or installed into the sides or window jambs?

Let's take these in order...

1. Designing your tile backsplash

The correct way to design a backsplash is to not let the outlet, switches or any obstacles overlapping the décor part of the tile design. To do so means detailing and laying out your pattern on paper long before you start the project.

Most tile is a nominal size, which means a 4"×4" tile isn't 4"×4"; chances are it's actual measurement might be 3¾" or 3⅞" (the manufacturers are assuming grout will take care of the difference in size).

If you can, order samples of your tile. (The pieces can be used in the actual design for later.) Lay it out on the table or a flat surface. Tile setters sometimes refer to this as a "dry lay".

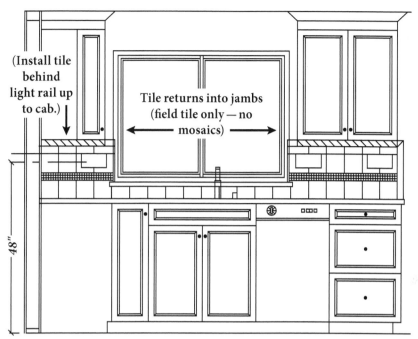

Providing a center height of outlets informs both the electrician and tile installer.

Do you have:

1) **Any protruding tiles or tile trim?** Some thicker are thicker than the rest of the tile. Others have a beveled edge or an uneven texture. These are the pieces you don't want your outlet to overlap.

2) **A decorative band or tile piece that is centered in the design?** Most outlets are centered on the backsplash between 6"–12" above the counter height. If your tile design has a protruding tile or a special detail, then your drawing of the plan will point out early whether or not to raise or lower either the electrical or the design.

3) **A tile that doesn't have any end pieces?** Most tiles are rough or unfinished on the edges. A really inexpensive tile only has the standard sizes without any end or finishing pieces "called "bullnose edge" or quarter round" or simply "trim pieces", — extra pieces of tile that are rounded or glazed on one or more edges — which are used in the design.

4) **Order more of hand-made tiles.** Expect color variations and order extra tile. What many people don't know is that the trim pieces might be made and painted in a different batch on an entirely different day from the rest of the backsplash tiles. In addition, the person who painted the trim isn't likely to be the same person who painted the subway tile. Ordering pieces later might only compound this issue, as you might be ordering yet another batch entirely.

Tile & Window detail: If you're planning on wrapping the tile into the sides of the window (some home plans only specified sheetrock instead of jambs and casing), be aware that the tile will create a smaller opening—and your existing blinds won't fit.

---

2. Stop your outlets from hogging the limelight

Let's say your backsplash is one that would do much better without a bank of outlets by the window. In fact, they mar your nice deco design, your bull nose trims, and just about everything. They're the wrong color, the wrong shape, and you wish they weren't there. And let's face it, there's nothing more glaring than the incorrect (or bright color) outlet. Fortunately, there are a couple of solutions to eliminate the outlets from the backsplash. (There's no option for the light switches; they'll have to be relocated.) Like all custom ideas, these aren't all standard solutions — they take a bit of thought and design work, and if your installers or your electrician aren't familiar with them, you might run into some difficulty without prior coordination.

- There are angled outlet strip plugs, thin boxes with multiple outlets that can be mounted underneath the cabinet, or even added to the underside of an island counter.
- There are also outlets that can be installed in the counter, but check both the outlets for kitchen use and your local building department to see if they allow their use.

- If your countertop is granite, there are granite switch plates and outlet plates available. Check with your local granite fabricator or check online for a matching "granite switch plates."
- Paint the outlet and switch covers with a faux finish to match the backsplash (if your painting skills aren't up to the challenge, look to your local specialty painters who deal with faux finishes.)

3. Or make them the stars

You know the old saying, "if you can't beat them, join them." There are times when a kitchen will only be partially remodeled, and the outlets and switches are there to stay. We don't have the luxury (or can bear the extra cost) of minimizing our outlets and switches.

So what do you do?

If you can't hide them, show them off. The actual switch and outlets themselves can't be changed easily, but their covers can. Decorative plate covers are designed in a variety of materials and colors, ranging from metals to bold ceramics.

First of all, know that there are two styles of switches and outlets — one is the older toggle switch (the plate has a small rectangular hole the size of your thumb joint) and the dual outlets are separate; the other is a newer style called Decora, where the switch is a fat rocker (the hole is the size of a small fist) and the dual outlets have a single rectangular plate joining them together.

While the actual toggle and rocker switch has to remain in the basic colors, there are other options for the plate covers. Look for "decorative switch plates" online. And the best part is that anyone with a screwdriver can change them very easily.

Under cabinet switch? I've heard of people mounting their switches on the underside of a wall cabinet, but that solution may not fly with the local building inspector or pass local codes. Check first.

4. Avoid backsplash "teeter–totters"

In this case, we're talking tiles — these are the cover plates installed on tiles that are uneven or have some embossed detail on them which prevents a cover plate from being installed correctly. *Here's what to watch for:*

a) **Tiles with beveled edges or ornate textures.** How will you fill in the bevel gap behind the outlet plate? *A solution might be to add a section of square tiles at each outlet or switch plate, just at those areas.*

A perfect example of a tile that'd make an electrician weep. For this tile, I'd suggest a flat tile cut in for the outlets, or an alternate method of outlets that aren't installed on a backsplash.

b) **Uneven, handmade tiles.** If your walls are out, the unevenness might show up more. *Lay out the tiles on the floor and select the straighter ones for the outlet and switch plate areas.*

c) **Embossed tiles.** Some tiles have raised design patterns on them, making them a challenge to mount outlets on. *Position them above or below the outlet, or design one square, flat tile to install the switch plate or outlet on.*

5. Let's talk grout

Yes, there's a skill in laying tile, but there's even a greater skill in mixing and setting grout. Surprising, isn't it? Yet, the type of water you have, how much humidity is in the room, and how the grout is mixed all contribute to the durability and final color rendering of the grout.

Here's what to watch for if you've never selected grout before or you want to do-it-yourself:

1) **You'll be lucky if the color matches the sample stick:** Really, the small sample sticks sit in dusty showrooms, someone's car, out to jobsites — the works. That the final color bears any resemblance to the sticks is a feat of skill by your tile-setters. When I'm selecting the grout color, I tend to go a shade darker than the true grout stick match — grout in a warm climate dries faster and turns out lighter than the stick.

2) **Make sure the bag is sifted and/or mixed before adding water:** Sometimes in shipping, the minerals/color can separate. If the color's either on the top or the bottom, and you use the rest of the bag later for the same project, you'll be wondering who switched the color when you weren't looking! If you have two bags, dry mix them together before starting. That way, if one bag is slightly different (it can happen), you've evened out the color.

3) **Follow the directions:** Almost every newbie with their first grout job thinks, "What's so hard about this? You mix grout powder with water — big deal" and ends up with crumbly grout popping out of the tile within a year.

4) **Watch your room temperature/humidity:** Just like in baking, how much water you add depends on room temperature, high humidity and/or altitude. Too little water and you end up with overly crumbly grout; too much water and it's runny. Grout that dries too quickly dries several shades lighter. In warmer/dryer climes, re-wetting the grout by wet towels slows down the curing process.

5) **Is your water hard or soft?** Both hard water (water with high mineral content) and excessive chlorine can also cause color variations. If you know your water is less than stellar, consider purchasing purified water or at least invest in a good water softener.

Sanded vs. un-sanded grout: If the grout line is less than ⅛" thick, use un-sanded. I might avoid sand for anything that can scratch—glass, marble, and metals like stainless steel. Check the tile manufacturer's specifications if you're unsure.

6. How does the splash thickness affect your appliances and plumbing?

If you're planning a thick backsplash — perhaps a ¾" stone or thicker type of tile installation that makes the total tile depth 1" thick — pay attention to what that creates behind a cook top or faucet.

Thickness like this will affect how far you can slide in a range, and with some models, leave a gap between the back of the range and the splash. It also takes away depth which might affect your cook top cut-out or cause your faucet difficulty. This is one of the reasons I ask my clients to select their tile, plumbing fixtures, and appliances early so I can spot tight fits before they happen.

Which leads us to our next topic, plumbing.

CHAPTER 11

FAUCET WEDGIES AND
OTHER PLUMBING OVERSIGHTS

The explosion of different sized sinks and smartly styled faucets has completely changed the design of the regular sink/clean-up space in recent years, yet it's not covered in most design books. And explosion is right. The sinks have become larger, deeper and wider. Plumbing fixtures from soap dispensers to separate hot and cold water dispensers have created a veritable city both on the counter and below the sink.

Unfortunately, standard counters and cabinets haven't yet grown along with this trend, and not all sinks and plumbing fixtures can be used together.

Faucet wedgies — really?

Once upon a time, sinks were approximately 16" deep, which left plenty of room in a regular 24" deep sink cabinet (22½" interior depth) for the faucet. Today's sinks vary between 18"–21" deep. This means one of two things — you'll either need to sharpen your pencils and math skills, or you can find out the hard way exactly what I mean by wedgie.

If you have a drop-in or self-rimming sink (they have a "lip" around the top of the sink that rests on the countertop), you're safe — it includes a decking at the back of the sink for the faucet and other plumbing fixtures.

But add a 21" deep under mount sink, and a 2½" diameter for the faucet, and you might be out of luck. (Note that these are the top measurements, which don't allow any extra space required for the fixtures to be bolted to the counter in the first place.) Even if you manage to squeeze them in, the faucet lever might hit the wall or the window sill, or the hot water dispenser could hug the wall so closely that there's no possible way to even squeeze your fingers behind all the fixtures, never mind clean back there.

An example of a faucet wedged between wall and sink. If this had been a side-lever, there would have been some pinched fingers.

Another factor most people miss is what the final thickness of the backsplash will be. A molded laminate backsplash is 1". A granite splash is ¾". Depending on your tile installation type (thin–set or mortar) and the thickness of your tile, you may need anywhere from ⅜" to 1". Now your 22½" of interior cabinet space really is 21½". This simply isn't enough room for most larger–scale sinks.

Hence, faucet wedgies — cramming too many products into a small space without checking the specifications first.

Here's a "save–your–kitchen" tip: standard 24" deep sink cabinets aren't usually deep enough for an 18" front–to–back under mount sinks and lever–style faucet, especially if the sink is placed against a sink window wall or a bar top. In this case, I'd recommend ordering a 27" deep sink cabinet. Again, this adds extra cost to your kitchen (a stone top must be also "bumped out"). Avoid doing this with a laminate top as the counter would be pieced in seamed sections — not the best place when water can damage those seams.

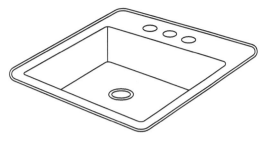

The flange for the faucet is the widest portion at the back of the sink, with 1 to 3 pre-drilled holes. (The 3-hole is shown here.)

1–or 3–holes in the sink? *One of my friends remodeling her kitchen counter had no idea that sinks come with multiple holes for the plumbing fixtures until she bought a new sink and faucet:*

A traditional faucet with separate hot and cold handles requires 3–holes at the top of the sink: one for the hot water handle, one for the cold water handle, and one for the faucet.

If your faucet has a single lever (the hot and cold can be blended depending on how you turn the handle) and this handle is attached to the faucet, then you only need to purchase a sink with 1 hole.

She bought the wrong one (she had a separate hot and cold levers) and a sink with one hole. She returned it for the 3–hole.

The difference between sink–mounted and deck–mounted faucets

On the self–rimming sink we've just been discussing, the faucet and other fixtures are referred to as "sink-mount". A deck–mount faucet is mounted on the countertop instead of the sink which is the case for all under mount and many apron sinks.

If you're planning for a lot of plumbing fixtures, make sure there are enough holes on the self-rimming sinks.

If you need to save money or the budget is tight, go with a self-rimming or drop-in sink. Here's why — an exposed counter edge such as the sink cut-out must be either polished (if it's stone or quartz or solid surfacing) or finished with the same material (if it's tile). This costs more. With a self-rimming sink, once it's dropped into the opening, it hides the cut-out edges.

What if you need more than 3 holes in your sink?

Some sinks offer 4–or 5–holes. This is important when the sink has a flange and offers the options of mounting the sink both under and over the counter. They might end their specification number with the number of holes. Thus, "Item 53128–4" has 4 holes.

In a stainless steel sink, some of these holes might be "plugs" (also called a "mounting hole") — extra holes covered over which you can't see from the top of the sink, but are readily apparent if you turn the sink over. They're meant to be popped or cut-out for use as needed.

If you need more than 5 holes for plumbing fixtures (faucet, hot water dispenser, air gap in some locations, soap dispenser, and air switch or second soap dispenser), then perhaps a self–rimming sink isn't for you — consider selecting a different sink which doesn't have this flange. (This works best with stone, tile, or solid surfacing.)

My fail-safe method for avoiding faucet wedgies:
1. Decide on the sink, faucet, and other plumbing fixtures you want, but do not buy them...yet.
2. Go to the manufacturer's websites and download all the technical specifications.
3. Read them thoroughly, especially the fine print. Does your sink say it needs any clearance at the front to install? What are the exact measurements of your faucet and the handles when they're turned on? (Lever–style handles are the worst culprits.)

4. Draw it all out to scale on graph paper.
(1 inch = 1 foot or any scale you want.)

5. Draw in the window sill (if you have one).

6. Draw in the raised bar top or raised counter
behind the sink (if you have one).

7. Draw in the thickness of your backsplash.

8. Add up all your measurements—does it all fit? If so,
congratulations. Now's the time to buy your fixtures.

9. Not sure? Check with your plumber or contractor.

A final thought on faucet wedgies

The new sinks are too deep to install a tilt-front drawer face in front of the sink to hold the sponges and scrubbers. If you want one, you'll need to choose a sink with a front-to-back depth of 16" or less.

What you might miss about stone/quartz counters and sink fabrication

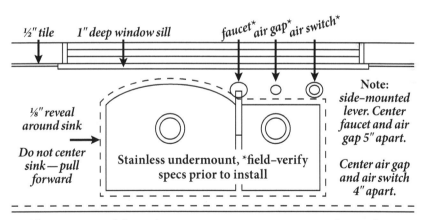

This is my typical design layout—prevents expensive misunderstandings or mistakes in on-site faucet drilling and placement.

If you're planning a stone counter, be aware that counter fabricators could use some guidance on where you'd like your sink placed. I've had some fabricators install sinks perfectly centered between the front edge and back wall, with equal distance between both points — not much help if I'm already battling faucet wedgies. In many cases, the sink needs to be "pulled forward" closer to the cabinet doors rather than the wall. You can't assume that the fabricator or person cutting out the sink will know your preferences. Talk to them first. Or make a note that you'd like to have the sink pulled forward in your sink layout diagram.

How many fixtures can you add to a sink?

The answer is as many as you want, but you may want to get a wider sink cabinet. As one of my plumbing friends noted, "Between the filtration cartridges for the water purifier, the tank for the hot water heater, the disposal and the rest, it starts resembling a small city under the sink!"

In addition to the faucet, there can be:

- **A water dispenser**. These can be either for hot water, filtered water, or a combination of both. I've specified both the separate hot water dispenser and separate filtered water on the same sink layout.
- **A hand spray**. Although many faucets now incorporate them, there are some styles that don't lend themselves to an integrated sprayer (or nozzle, depending on your regional terms).
- **A soap dispenser**. Can be for dish–or hand–soap.
- **An air switch**. An air switch is a button mounted on the countertop that pushes air down to a switch which turns the garbage disposal on. It is used in place of a wall switch using compressed air to activate.

Some locations, like California, also require a dishwasher air gap to prevent siphoning or back–flow of dirty water back into the dishwasher (an air tube runs from the metal piece on the counter to the disposal.)

Do you need to center the sink under the window?

This is one of those "this is the way it's always been done" kitchen myths I discussed in the first chapter, and how traditions and perceived values play a large part in home design long after the original reason no longer exists.

The original reason was light.

Or, to put it another way: lack of electricity. My grandparents had a ranch dating back to early homesteading days. My grandmother performed the majority of her food prep where the light was–at the kitchen sink. (At night, there were kerosene lamps and cut-throat card–players at the kitchen table, but that's another story...)

Windows also weren't the size they are today. Early glass was poured, not molded, making it fragile, and expensive. It didn't travel well over long distances (which is why you see so many panes in heritage buildings; the smaller panes were easier to transport) which meant smaller windows that were no more than 24" to 30" wide. In early apartments, they weren't located over the sink area, either.

Fast forward to today. We have round the clock electricity and new methods of glass–making. Our kitchen windows in new homes are no longer 30" — they're now 36" to 96" wide.

A lot of my clients say, "Well, I like to look out the window when I'm at the sink." Fine. But should you still center a sink in a 60"-96" window? After all, if you're selecting a sink style that is a bowl and a half (big bowl/ small bowl configuration), your faucet is going to be off-set to the left or right anyway.

As a thought, can you consider locating it to one side and use the counter space for decent work surface? It works very well in some kitchens, and not in others.

Five facts about garbage disposals

1) Check your local building codes to see if they allow garbage disposals (known as garbeurator or garburator in Canada). Not all do.
2) There are mixed opinions about using a disposal with a septic tank. Part of the argument has to do with climate, location, and what can be disposed of. Check with your local plumber.
3) A disposal is not meant to be a garbage can.
4) Use running cold water when using the disposal. Hot water can overheat some motors.
5) Don't turn off disposal before it has finished grinding.

Like the idea of a soap dispenser but hate filling it?

Most of my clients were ambivalent about adding a soap dispenser because the bottle for the soap was mounted under the dispenser, behind the sink bowl, and usually so small that it needed to be changed often. My favorite solution for this is to add a Mountain soap dispenser tube. This is an adaptive tube which screws both into the soap dispenser and any soap container you buy. (The bottle that comes with your dispenser can be eliminated.) Now you can buy larger container of soap so it lasts longer, and you don't have to crawl into the cabinet to add more soap — the container simply sits on the cabinet floor.

Hot water dispensers might drip once in awhile.

If your hot water dispenser leaks a drop or two every so often, there's a good reason. It helps relieve the pressure in the hot water tank. If the water tastes odd or bad, you may need to add a water filter. If you live at a higher elevation, you may have to lower the temperature. These, and many other details, can usually be found in the "trouble–shooting" portion of your manuals. These are the ones that garner the most questions from my readers.

A thought on apron sinks

An apron sink, also known as a farmhouse sink, is a style where the front part of the sink (or apron) is exposed. There is no top false door panel; the sink "sits" on top of the cabinet and/or may have a front panel that is cut out to accept the sink.

Spills and splashes of everyday water use sometimes trickle down the front of the sink and wind up on the cabinet doors below. Over time, this leads to water damage of both wood–stained and painted cabinets. It wasn't an issue in the original days of farm house sinks because the sinks didn't have cabinets below. They were often propped on legs with the space hidden by a curtain.

So here's a trick to save the paint from peeling or the stain to wear off the cabinet doors below the apron sink. Add a small half-round trim directly below the sink and above the sink doors.

This is called a drip dam and while it's no guarantee against consistent drips, it will stop the majority of water trickling from the sink to the cabinet. Custom cabinets may have this piece included as part of the apron sink cabinet design, or a cabinet-maker may add it. It's an easy solution even if you have stock cabinets — simply order one piece of extra trim piece, such as a half-round piece ¾"-1" thick with the cabinets and install on-site.

An apron sink without the trim (drip dam) between the sink and the doors below. The rounded top edge of the sink makes it easy for the water to drip over the edge.

If it becomes water-damaged, it's easy enough to remove and replace compared to replacing the water-damaged doors later on.

Corner sinks

This isn't about pushing the sink as close to the corner as possible, although there are elements to watch for with that design. I'm also not talking about a true angled sink with both bowls at a 90-degree angle. This is about placing a standard large bowl, or double-bowl sink diagonally in the corner.

The benefit is that it eliminates a corner — which is not our favorite area for storage — in order to gain the prime frontage space that a sink typically uses. Some plans have corner windows or no windows at all.

On the downside, it's definitely a one-person working area and challenging to get two people in there if you need a wash-dry team. Cooks with lower back problems would feel the strain of working at the sink for longer periods of time since there's a slight twisting motion as one reaches for dishes on the counter.

If you're planning on a diagonal sink, here's what you need to know:

a) **It works best with a semi-custom, an in-house build, or custom cabinet line:** Don't install a standard straight cabinet in the corner. It puts the person washing at the sink almost a full 54" away from the back corner. It's not only a waste of a corner, but if you're not tall, you'll be climbing on the counter and over the faucet to clean that section of counter behind them.

b) **If the cabinet company has a diagonal sink corner, how wide can the sink be?** Some might only fit a single-bowl 24" sink. Again, watch the size — if you want large double or triple sinks, this isn't the design for you. Even recessing or pushing the cabinet back into the corner has its pros and cons — it will create sharp corners at either side of the sink (and will add extra fabrication cost to your counters).

c) **A small double-sink or single sink works best:** A 42" wide angled cabinet (42" both ways on the back wall; the angled corner door will be approx. 24" wide depending if the cabinets are frame or frameless) works best for design but not for the plumber who has to set the sink in the corner — the sides of the cabinet will need to be cut out at the front to accommodate a 32" wide sink. If you really have your heart set on a sink larger than that, then a corner sink design might not be your best option.

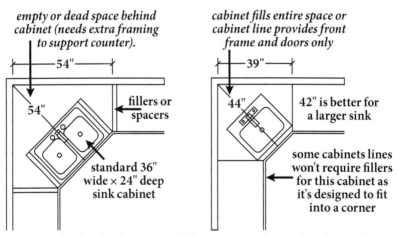

empty or dead space behind cabinet (needs extra framing to support counter).

—54"—

54"

fillers or spacers

standard 36" wide × 24" deep sink cabinet

cabinet fills entire space or cabinet line provides front frame and doors only

—39"—

44"

42" is better for a larger sink

some cabinets lines won't require fillers for this cabinet as it's designed to fit into a corner

The standard sink cabinet installed in a corner takes up lot of space, both in width and depth. A 39"–42" angled cabinet might be a challenge for a plumber to install the sink, but it definitely saves more space.

There's another factor to watch when designing a sink in the corner — what happens to the dishwasher? That's what we'll talk about in the next chapter...

CHAPTER 12

COLD, WET TRUTHS ABOUT REFRIGERATORS AND DISHWASHERS

Some of the costliest "didn't–think–through" errors are with appliances — especially refrigerators and dishwashers. It doesn't help that there are hundreds of models in varying sizes and styles and all requiring different methods of installation.

There's not much of an issue with "standard" refrigerators and dishwashers; it's the custom units which require complicated installation or factory–trained installers or custom cabinet doors and panels for an integrated look.

In this chapter, we'll discuss both what you need to know about the appliances themselves, and how some of the major styles can affect your kitchen layout.

How will you know what to watch for?

There are 4 basic styles of appliances, which range from low to high, simple to complex: in cost, options, and installation/design time.

Let's start with the basics:

1) **Standard.** In this case, a standard dishwasher or refrigerator means a unit which fits in the most popular widths and heights, with only the simplest of installations (slide in and hook–up/plug–in). Refrigerators are 32"–36" wide × 71" high. Dishwashers are 24" wide. Cabinet

modifications aren't necessary. Each is the easiest unit to buy as a replacement for an existing kitchen and the simplest to fit into a stock kitchen.

2) **Mid-range.** This is the next step up and might include some extra options that standard units don't have — such as a flange on the door to hold cabinet door panels to the face or the refrigerators might be counter deep at 24"–25" deep. These require a bit more time to install if there are cabinet panels to be installed.

3) **Luxury.** These are the built-in refrigerators, which are 84" high. They might also include refrigerator or dishwasher drawer units. Many of these require factory-trained installers to install (in order to maintain the warranty), and extra hours to design and install. While one can use stock cabinets, not all stock cabinet lines may have the right parts.

4) **Ultra-luxury.** These are the most expensive of appliances, the type that require assembly on-site. They might be a refrigerator that looks like a pantry, or a 36" wide dishwasher door. At the opposite end of standard, these units look completely built in. The amount of time to install might take over a day. I know of one refrigerator where the doors come separately and must be carefully counter-balanced in place. It is almost impossible to use stock cabinets for these lines, because the customization of the door panels is so great.

Check the appliances for damage as soon as they come into your home, and make a note (or inform the delivery person if you spot something during unloading). There is only a short window of opportunity to stake your claim on damages, and if you take too long, it becomes a real challenge to prove your case later.

Appliances increase in price every year: Find out when your manufacturer is planning an increase (I check with my local appliance showrooms). Sometimes it's a significant difference. If you know that you're going to build your house in the spring

and your appliance prices are increasing after the new year,
ask if you can pay early to hold the pricing.

Dishwashers (the non–human, non–complaining type)
Four typical design mistakes to avoid

The first dishwashers weren't installed under the counter. You wheeled them up to the sink, hooked up a hose, and turned on the hot water. The dishwasher was so noisy, you couldn't hear yourself think. My mother used to say it was still quieter than her children. (Thanks, mom.)

Today's new dishwashers are quiet and sleek. They are available in units that take up an entire 24" of space under the counter, or they can come as single or dual 24" wide drawers which can be mounted together or installed as separate units. There's even a 36" drawer unit available.

Whatever the size or shape, here are 3 things people get stuck on:

a) **Installing a thicker floor but keeping the existing cabinets.** We'll discuss this later on in flooring, but this is too sadly common. Homeowner decides to replace only the thinner vinyl floor with a thicker wood and discovers the dishwasher will no longer fit under the counter. Don't let this happen to you. Check to see if the dishwasher has the clearance height and what the new flooring will take away before you buy.

b) **People forget the walk path around an open dishwasher door (or drawer.)** There is a reason we draw the openings of all appliance doors on a floor plan — it helps us spot where that door might impede the traffic or strike against other opened doors.

c) **Installing a dishwasher too far away from the sink.** Depending on your local codes, the distance between the sink and dishwasher centers shouldn't be greater than five feet. Check with your local codes.

Design your dishwasher away from an angle

Placing a dishwasher next to an angled corner, with no separation between them might cause a couple of outcomes — the dishwasher handle or door might effectively bind the drawers and doors beside it from opening and the open dishwasher door might leave no space for someone to stand at the sink.

Cramming cabinets and appliances into an angle without space or fillers is a fairly common mistake. Move your cabinets and dishwashers away from the angle — at least 1½" per side if the cabinet is frameless. That's the minimum and doesn't account if your dishwasher has one of those big architectural handles which requires more than that. **1**

For standard dishwashers with protruding top control panels, I leave 3" both ways. (Many stock cabinets have fillers or spaces that are only 3" wide), again if it's a standard, non–integrated dishwasher.

However if possible, I prefer to leave at least 12"–21" wide of space between the angle and the dishwasher (15" wide and larger will provide enough room for a cutlery drawer).

This allows enough space for a bank of drawers between the angle and dishwasher, but more importantly, there's now enough walking room between the lowered dishwasher door and the other angled wall of cabinets. This allows room for unloading and loading the dishwasher from both sides of the dishwasher — although it's still a bit tight if someone's at the sink. **2**

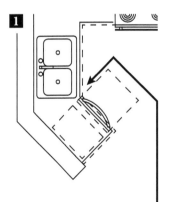

A dishwasher installed too close to the angle which doesn't leave enough room to stand by the sink when the door is open.

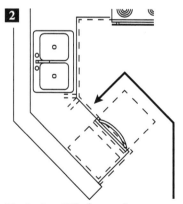

Designing 15" of space between the dishwasher and the corner provides room to unload on the right side of the d/w. More importantly, the extra cabinet space adds cutlery storage right where we need it.

Dishwasher integrated door panels —
two tips to prevent re-ordering door panels

An integrated door panel is simply a door panel ordered with the cabinets to attach to the dishwasher face. Once applied, the dishwasher face ends up looking like the rest of the cabinets.

Here are two tips I've learned the hard way:

a) Pay close attention to the dishwasher and check the models before you buy — in order for the hinging to work, the door panel ends up hanging below the rest of the cabinet doors.

b) If the specification sheet isn't 100% clear, then hold off ordering the cabinet panels until the dishwasher is installed. Yes, it might delay finishing the project, but you also might save paying for multiple doors if you didn't read the specifications correctly the first time. In some cases, I wait until the appliances are installed and on-site, because the specifications weren't correct.

Installing a new dishwasher in existing cabinets and counters?
Better check the depth!

Right up until the 1990s, some cabinets built in-house were only 23¼" — 24" deep with a 24" deep counter top, which means most of today's dishwashers (which are deeper than that) won't fit flush with your existing cabinets or counter.

If you wish to keep your existing old-depth counters and cabinets, here's a way to check first: Measure the countertop from front to back. If the counter itself is 24" (or even 24½") and not today's standard of 25"–26" (standard: 25½"), then you have an older style cabinet.

If you can't stand the thought of the door protruding, take a look at European dishwashers: some are shallower in depth by an inch or so than our regular North American dishwashers.

Refrigerators

I sometimes think that our jobs would be a lot easier if there were both fewer models and that the existing models weren't tweaked for design so often.

So what happens is that beginners and/or first–time remodelers get caught with not thinking through the details. Pros get caught off–guard with designs or re–tweaking by the manufacturers for existing models. ("Look, our consumers were asking for bigger shelves on our refrigerator door. We can't help it if we forgot to mention it, and the old width for accessing the crisper needs to be wider. Sorry. You tell the client.")

Leave extra width for your standard refrigerator

Not all refrigerators have straight sides and might even bow out slightly. This might be due to design, shipping, or any number of causes. I've rarely seen it happen with luxury refrigerators; however, if you're ordering a standard refrigerator:

- *If the refrigerator is on–site:* Measure the width of the refrigerator case at three points: base, middle, and top.
- *If the widths all match, you're fine. If the refrigerator isn't in before the cabinets are ordered:* Allow some extra width to your opening (between ¼"–½" max.) Don't forget to add that width to your refrigerator cabinet width above — either with a filler or customization.

How French door refrigerators fight with American–style design

A French door refrigerator is one where the refrigeration section has a set of double–doors, with a freezer door below them. This is unlike a side–by–side refrigerator, where the right refrigerator door is opened constantly, but the left freezer door is only opened occasionally. Both doors of a French door style must be opened at the same time to access larger platters or case goods.

When this new style of refrigerator debuted, no one ever thought of the design implications of both doors fully opened.

We needed more space between a side wall and the refrigerator…on both sides. The counter–depth refrigerators (those that were only 24" deep) caused the most problems as counters were deeper than the refrigerator. Unless the counter corner next to the refrigerator was beveled or angled, the opened refrigerator door would strike against the sharp corner with unfortunate results.

The same thing happened for designing built–in ovens in tall cabinets next to the shallower depth refrigerators. No matter which side we installed the ovens, there was a good possibility one of the refrigerator door would hit against the oven handles. We needed to change our design tactics in order to make this French style work.

A designer solution

If the refrigerator cabinet and side panel hadn't been "bumped out", either the counter or the knobs from the pantry would have collided with (and damaged) the opened refrigerator doors.

Increase the depth of the side re-frigerator panels and the cabinet above to 27" deep. Now the counter dies (a trade definition meaning it ends or butts into the side of an-other item) into the side panel so the left refrigerator door won't hit it. The same thing applies to the right door — if the refrigerator hadn't been pulled forward slightly, the cabinet knobs on the pantry on the right would have made 2 fine dents on the opened refrigerator door.

A thought on refrigerator ice and water dispensers

Whether you think they're the greatest invention since the wheel, or the very thought of owning one makes you shiver, one of the biggest regrets about ice and water dispensers is that few of us get to test them before buying. It's only after it's installed that we discover they're all different in the way they dispense. Some are gentle; others are rapid-fire and high-stream.

What it means to you depends on your lifestyle, your flooring materials, and your sanity. No matter how careful we might be, sometimes mistakes happen. If someone in your household isn't careful about mopping up water or ice-cubes that overshoot his or her glass, eventually that extra melting ice or water on your floor will lower the life expectancy of you (as you slip) or your floor (if it's wood).

Ask the appliance specialist if they've heard anything about the dispensers of the refrigerator you like. Check for reviews. Best of all, know how your family will use them. That may be the most telling detail of all.

Appliance Color Tip: A white (or off-white) appliance in one brand may be a slightly different shade or tone in another brand. It's done deliberately so you'll only buy one brand. Verify the colors prior to purchasing.

Don't forget to include the refrigerator hinge to the overall height

Every so often, someone wanders into the showroom with a fairly common problem: they're keeping the existing cabinets and bought a new refrigerator...which doesn't fit under the existing wall cabinet.

Here's what has happened. Many of the refrigerators that were 68" high a decade ago are now 71"–72" high. The newer refrigerators are simply too big.

Don't let this happen to you. It's especially important if the cabinet above the refrigerator is 24" or deeper (it doesn't pertain so much to a 12" deep cabinet — the refrigerator hinge usually clears. I haven't heard of someone opening a 12" cabinet door and hitting the hinge, but it would depend on the cabinet style).

Here are three details to watch for:

a) **The height of the refrigerator should include hinges.** Every specification I know usually includes hinge height.

b) **Is your floor level?** I used to own a home from 1906; the surprise was when areas *were* level. If your floor rises at any point under the refrigerator, you're still left with the same problem: the refrigerator won't fit. Leave at least ½ inch; an inch is better. Best yet: check the refrigerator specifications; they'll usually state the measurements you need.

c) **Any plans for adding a new floor in the future?** This is like the dishwasher story. Solid wood is thicker than vinyl, tile with the mortar beds can be thicker than wood. If you're going to re–do your floors down the road, allow for the new height now. I've designed kitchens where we've installed vinyl for the early baby years, and then installed the wood flooring for the client some years later.

A solution:

If you're planning to order cabinets and they're not going to be custom, here's what I might suggest:

Order the refrigerator cabinet with 3" of room to spare between the top of the refrigerator hinge and the underside of the cabinet. Order a separate valance, and install it underneath the cabinet using removable angle or "L"–shape brackets. That way, if the refrigerator or your floor changes height, the valance can be removed or trimmed to fit. Problem solved.

Remember the tip for leaving space beside an angled corner? That goes double for refrigerators.

Refrigerators are deeper than all other appliances, up to a maximum of 34" deep with the handle. Even the "built–in" refrigerators still protrude further than a 24" deep once we allow for the electrical plug and counters and side panels. How the doors swing also determine whether they'll pinch against a corner.

The last refrigerator I placed next to a lazy susan, I allowed 15" of swing space to the adjacent counter. The design was hindered by the kitchen door to the garage, which wouldn't allow us any more movement away from the corner. So I designed with the understanding that according to the appliance specifications, 14" of clearance width to the corner was sufficient.

Except it wasn't and the specifications were incomplete. Any time the door swung wider than 135–degrees, it hit against the counter and eventually had to be redesigned.

When you design the refrigerator next to the corner, ask how wide you will be swinging the door open before you make your final decision…and allow more than what the specifications say.

Under counter Refrigeration

This type of refrigeration includes bar refrigerators which includes beverage centers or wine captains, refrigerator drawers, and ice–makers.

Most icemakers require a water line and a drain

These ice–makers (sometimes referred to as "free–standing") are individual units which mount the same way as any under counter appliance (and are similar in size to a trash compactor). The biggest difference is that they require a dedicated cold water supply line with appropriate pressure. They also require a drain or a condensate pump, depending on the manufacturer requirements.

If they need a drain, perhaps those of you who have a concrete slab floor might want to re–think your design unless the plans for your new home allow for installing a drain in advance.

Check the height of the under counter refrigerator/wine captain before you buy: For a few years, some manufacturers were making under counter wine and beverage centers 35¼" high with adjustment. The standard height to the underside of the counter is 34½" high. They're slowly coming around, but in the meantime, check the height specification before you buy.

CHAPTER 13

SIZZLING TIPS FOR RANGES, COOK TOPS, AND OVENS

In the demand for "pro" appliances, cooking appliances have undergone the most radical changes of all appliances. Whether they're gas, standard electric, magnetic induction, convection, or microwave, each still has a quirk or two when it comes to installation, heating, and ventilation elements. While the future of these appliances will feature more of the finger touch controls or visual screens to call up popular recipes, ultimately they'll still have the same challenges as all the rest — safety.

When dealing with heat, we require extra care focusing on the operation of the doors for both appliances and the cabinets around them.

In this chapter, we'll look at what happens when these appliances are placed around the room, and some of the beginning mistakes that most people don't think of when selecting these units.

Cook tops and Range tops

Before we start with the doors, let's start with the heat — cook tops and range tops. Here's how a designer sees them:

1) **Gas.** How powerful is the unit and what do the specifications say for the minimum distance between the burners and adjacent flammable materials? Will the backsplash need to be fire–proofed or will the material suffer at high heat?

2) **Electric:** Electric is the easiest of the group. It doesn't require overly powerful ventilation and since it doesn't provide as much heat as gas, also doesn't require as much distance between the heat and flammable objects. It's also the most inexpensive of the three.

3) **Induction:** How much power will the unit require and is the electrical panel big enough to accept it? Will the style allow for drawers underneath or will it require air space below the unit to the nearest shelf?

Cook top vs. range top—which is better for a young family?

One caveat I leave for clients with young children is that the professional gas tops are just that—very high heat elements that can cause instant third degree burns beyond what the typical electrical tops. If you really want gas, seriously think about how high the BTUs or British Thermal Units will be, and think about young hands reaching in areas their tiny owners can't see.

British Thermal Units are the amount of energy needed to heat 1 pound (0.454 kg) of water 1 °F (0.55 °C). The higher the BTUs, the hotter (and more powerful) your burners are.

Also think about the type of top: range top or cook top. It's easier for a child to reach the front controls of a range top than it is to reach the controls on top.

Insider Definition (Cook top vs. range top)

Cook top: Unit that is dropped into the top of a countertop and sits flat on the counter. The controls are on this surface.
Range top: Unit with the controls at the front, usually gas. The cabinet below must be customized to eliminate the top drawer front, which is where the controls fit.

My take on induction vs. gas

Simply put, induction cooks by electromagnetic field. When a metal pot is placed within the field, it generates heat. It's been used by the rest of the world for decades and we're getting caught up now.

I'd discussed this becoming a trend a few years back when I and my designer mother visited Las Vegas and saw one of the fancy restaurant kitchens using induction. (Where the professional chefs go, the rest of us aren't far behind...especially if our clients are foodies or serious cooks.)

Here's why it's going to gain in popularity over the next decade.
- 80% of the heat is transferred compared to 40% with gas.
- It's instant heat and as fast and as easy to control as gas.
- Less dangerous to little fingers because the elements are cool — the heat transfers to the pot. (There still might be some heat transfer from a hot pot, but it's never as hot as standard electrical or gas.)
- No intense heat generated from cooking which can be a boon to hotter climate homes.
- Much easier to clean than the gas top grills or electric rings.
- No need for as powerful ventilation as gas since there's no off–gassing, so it can be a boon for the newer sealed homes. A powerful hood removing all the air requires an intake elsewhere in to replace that air.
- Yes, you need pots that can work with the magnetic field, but you don't have to spend a fortune.

Where it might not be the best choice.
- If the home's electrical panel is full or there isn't enough power to the home. A typical 30" wide unit takes 40amp (similar to an oven); the 36"–42" wide units require almost 50amps — not a good thing if you only have 100 amp service.
- There are still some concerns about pace–makers affected by the magnetic field. I've done enough research to understand it's the type of

pacemaker that can make a difference, but do your research if this might be a concern.

- Some units require space underneath to the nearest shelf, which might limit pot drawers or storage space.

Designing a cook top/range top or range in the corner

I've certainly designed kitchens with the range and cook top in the corner, and I'll warn you now: while they're fine for large kitchens where there is plenty of space, they take more room (and design thought) than most people think.

A 30" cook top takes approximately 45"–48" of wall space both ways. A 36" will take about 51"–54" both ways.

That's simply for a cook top — the range top is a completely different kettle of fish. See how the unit protrudes past the cabinet and countertop?

The deeper control panel is typical for gas range tops. A full–height cabinet door installed on either side of this unit would take some damage if it was hinged incorrectly.

If your installation details aren't designed to the nth degree, the controls will provide a lovely stopper or door destroyer when you open the cabinets on either side of a angled range top. This is where fillers or spacers added between the cabinets on either side of the unit and the cabinet become an absolute necessity.

"No problem," you say. "There's room behind the range top. I'll push it back as far to the wall as possible."

There is no space savings — and now when the oven door is opened, there won't be any room to stand beside it. You'll need to pull the racks all the way out and reach in.

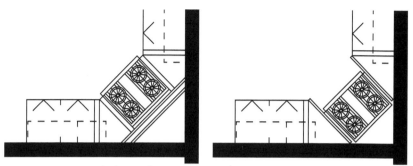

Doesn't do much except create hip–bangers and make the hood fan installation a real challenge.

What happens to the wall cabinets next to the hood fan?

Glad you asked. A hood fan protrudes anywhere from 16" to 27". The doors on the wall cabinets will not open beside a hood fan because they'll hit against the hood. If there's only enough space to install the top and hood into the corner, the wall cabinets on either side will have to be either open shelves or blind panels.

Here are some tips before you make your final decision:

If your absolute dream is to have a range or top in the corner and you believe you have room, here's what I suggest:

1) A cook top will give you the most options (vs. a range or a range top), and will be the easiest to install because it doesn't have a protruding face affecting the openings of the nearby cabinet drawers and doors. The most design work and arithmetic will come with the pro appliances.

2) Select your range or top, and hood, but don't purchase them yet. Before you buy, draw all the units either to scale on paper, or lay it out on the floor. Research the overall depths of your range top knobs, your oven handles, and finally, the drawer/door handles beside the appliance to determine what spacing is actually required.

3) Don't forget to add fillers or ears as blank panels in the corner. They can be as small as 1½" but 3" wide or more will prevent cabinet doors from swinging into the appliance face

4) Now draw any doors as "open" at their fullest. Cabinet doors swing 110–degrees.

If we kept our ovens and cook tops 24" wide like they do in Europe, we'd only take this amount of space instead of another third of wall space. Note how the hood angles back to avoid upper door collisions and the slight space between the oven and base doors for clearance.

I find when laying out the corner out on the sub–floor, clients are shocked both at how much room a corner appliance takes up, as well as how much room is wasted in the corners to make this work.

I use a chalk line which can be purchased at any lumber yard. Be careful using chalk if you're installing vinyl or using it on an already finished floor — the chalk can bleed through or stain. Cut some paper or cardboard and tape it together on the floor instead.

Can you install a gas oven under a cook top?

Almost all gas tops I'm familiar with have the gas inlet installed on the bottom of the unit and/or require stringent height requirements that would make it impossible to install a gas oven under a cook top or range top.

A quick glance at a couple of well-known gas oven specifications point out that that their recommended heights from the bottom of the oven to the floor should be 17" and 22" respectively. I don't know about you, but I doubt I can work on a counter that would end up at 48"–54" high! However, there's another point in the fine print: many gas ovens aren't allow for installation under counters, likely due to the high heat they exude during cooking.

What about an electric oven under a gas or electric cook top?

This configuration definitely has more options. In this case, the overall height of the oven needs to be +/– 26" high with a cook top that is +/– 4" high or any combination that amounts to 30" high or under. If the combination of the two is over 30" high, which is the height of the actual base cabinet without the recessed toe kick, the appliances won't fit. I can't provide an exact combination — all final answers will come from the specifications.

What about an electric oven mounted below an induction cook top?

Refer to the cook top specifications, as some allow this (with only certain brands — their own or some other specification) and some won't.

Some induction cook tops require an airspace between the underside of the cook top and a combustible surface, such as a shelf. An oven won't fit under these models. Check carefully before you buy.

Can I put a range or cook top under a window?

Of course, you can do whatever you want. However, why you might face serious resistance from professionals is the flammability issue of the material behind the cook top or range — the window jambs, curtains, or blinds.

You might swear up–and–down that the area will be tiled and you won't add a speck of curtain material…however that's tough to guarantee when the next homeowner moves in. They didn't hear all the disclaimers.

If you're considering a very high BTU range or top:
Some of these new high–heat gas ranges are hotter than blowtorches, and require special wall backing to protect your wood framing. (Those of you with brick or steel framing are better off.)

> If you're planning on the ultra–deluxe, most powerful BTU
> gas range or top on the market, plan your final backsplash
> materials with care. I have seen grout burn and some charring
> on the 2×4 studs behind the backsplash walls which leads me
> to suggest a) non–flammable concrete backer board instead
> of standard drywall, and b) selecting backsplash materials
> that can withstand high heat.

Also, professional gas ranges should be vented. There's a lot of gas fumes and smoke, some of which you could eliminate by cracking a window, but not all of it makes it outside, and spreads inside the home.

I've seen designs where a non–flammable 8"–12" backsplash was built behind the range and the window was installed above this and the design treatment was such so there would be no blinds or window treatments, but I usually see these in high–end remodels, and not in kitchens where the range is simply relocated under an existing window. If the range isn't super powerful, I can be swayed. Otherwise, professionals have seen too many scorch marks on walls to be comfortable with this as a standard. Forewarned is forearmed.

Hood Fans

Head–bangers or Spit–guards?
What you need to know about pro hoods

At one time, ventilation was a fan in the ceiling or a wall, which changed to the hood fans we see today. The only difference between the hoods of today and from 30–40 years ago is the big increase in depth. Under cabinet hoods are 16"–18" deep. Professional, or custom vents are 24"–27" deep.

This poses a dilemma: The engineers who design the venting ideally would like us to install hoods approximately 24"–30" off the counter for maximum performance. That's approximately 60"–66" off the floor— the height of my nose or a taller person's chin.

So we have a problem — do we sacrifice the ventilation capability by raising the hoods out of the way, or do we keep them low and hope for the best? Yes, this is dangerous. These hood fans are heavy and made out of superb stainless steel. I have heard stories of serious injuries from people hitting their heads on the front or corners of the hoods. Here's my answer: I've been specifying installing the professional hoods higher — between 69"–72" high off the floor — for a number of years now.

Always check the depth:

- If you're the main cook at 5'2" but need to raise the hood for a 6'0" significant other, can *you* still reach the controls? If not, you may want to consider a remote switch (ask your appliance person).
- If you're the main cook and you're taller than 6'0", you'll need to raise the hood higher. Of course, this depends on the existing ceiling height and the power of the hood. Raise it too high and you run the risk of it not working well. This is where I might suggest alternate options, such as the hoods that aren't as deep or at least have softened corners.

An example of a chimney-style hood over a peninsula. These hoods are 27"–30" deep. I wouldn't recommend this arch for someone tall unless we set the install height from the lowest points on the curve.

> **Custom Hood Tip:** Custom designer hoods (the ones you see
> made from wood or metal or faux finishes look too squat and
> out–of–balance in an 8 foot high kitchen. Most photos you see
> of custom hoods are in kitchens with 9 or 10 foot ceilings.

Professional Hoods — ducting and 2–story homes

Standard hood ducts used to be either 4" round or 4"×10" rectangular. The professional hood ducting is much bigger — often up to 10" round.

In a two–story home with the kitchen on the bottom floor, it means that the ducting is often installed up to the kitchen ceiling and in between the second–story ceiling joints to the nearest exterior wall.

If the joists are big enough, or run the opposite way to where the hood needs to be ducted, it becomes an installation problem that is solved only by either creating a soffit above the cabinets or possibly running the ducting through the wall cabinets — not something you want to discover after you've started your remodel!

> **Burned out hood light?** Don't go to a lighting store — they won't
> have them in stock. You'll need to order them from the appliance
> manufacturer or wherever you bought your appliances.

Can you install a 30" wide fan over a 36" cook top or range?

I avoid it if the burners are gas, and here's why: the standard wall cabinets on either side of the fan unit will end up partially installed over burners. 18" of space from the burners to the cabinets isn't enough — the cabinets will scorch over time. In fact, many cook top and range manufacturers have strict guidelines on the clearances between the gas burners and what they call "flammable materials" which in this case, would be your cabinets. Refer to the specifications first.

A warning on installing hood fans in sealed homes

Traditionally, the more powerful the gas range, the more powerful
the ventilation unit—which can pose a danger in the new sealed
homes. All removed air must be replaced, otherwise the ventilation
creates a vacuum in the home which can suck the flame out of gas
fireplaces or affect the workings of the existing air exchanger
system. If you have a sealed home, and want a powerful range, I
might suggest induction instead of pro gas. It won't require such a
high (and potentially dangerous) hood fan.

Microwaves

While I'd like to write a great deal about microwaves, there's not really
much to tell. Most standard microwaves hinge on the left side. There are
no right–hand swings.

There are 4 types of microwaves for design purposes:

a) **Standard:** Sits on the counter or in a shelf. Typically 12"–16" deep.
Some units have brackets to install the unit to the underside of the
wall cabinets.

b) **Convection/large:** Typically 16"–20" deep. Too deep (and heavy) to
fit on a shelf, and is best on a counter or in a tall pantry cupboard.

c) **Over–the–range:** Typically 12"–14" deep and combined with either
standard ventilation or re–circulating (there is no vent—the steam
passes through a charcoal filter and back into the room again).

d) **Drawer unit:** Some of the newer models resemble a warming drawer.
They're designed to be installed under the countertop.

One of the biggest disappointments for most microwaves is that the
standard depth is 16"–20" deep—a waste of good counter space or room in
a 24" deep oven cabinet, and too "in–your–face" when mounted under a wall
cabinet. They require a special depth shelf deeper than a typical 12" deep wall
cabinet. If this bothers you, decide what you want your microwave *for*. If
it's only for reheating or melting butter, I'll show you a 12" deep unit later on.

An example of a microwave cabinet extending to the counter. With a 16"–20" microwave, there's almost no counter left — the 12½" deep microwave would leave more counter in front of the cabinet.

Placing a microwave under the counter

One of the challenges of placing a standard microwave under the counter is that it's too low for most adults. In order to see what's inside the microwave, we bend lower than we think. Reaching for something heavy and hot is a challenge.

This is where the new microwave drawers are useful. They are indeed a drawer which makes accessibility easier for stirring and removal.

A nice bonus: the potential of food spills on the floor is eliminated, since we're now lifting items that spill over the drawer and not the floor.

Not every microwave is designed to fit over a cook top or range: Over–the–range or OTR microwaves have a fan unit built into them and are designed in such a way that the underside has both a light and some protection against heat.

Building a shelf to put a standard microwave over the range violates codes and could be a safety issue — even if you used a non–flammable metal shelf, a regular microwave is not built to take higher heat temperatures.

Another design idea for the microwave

If you have counter space, and you're planning on semi-custom or custom cabinets, consider a deeper wall cabinet which can extend down to the counter. The microwave can be set into cabinet but don't install it at counter level — opening the microwave door will sweep anything you have in front of the microwave onto the floor. Add one 6" high drawer between the microwave and counter, which will raise the microwave off the counter approximately one coffee cup high.

What is the microwave trim kit for?

In the early days, openings for oven units were rough and unfinished, or often cut on site. They allowed for circulation around the microwave itself.

Today's trim kits are used to make a microwave look the same width as an oven when used in an oven cabinet, but in some luxury homes, the cabinets are custom designed, which eliminates the need for the trim kit. Read the specifications — many microwaves still require air circulation around the units, whether it's extra width at the opening, or ventilation holes drilled on the bottom of the shelf.

Need a 12" deep microwave to fit under your 12" wall cabinet?

There's only one brand that most of the designers I know like to specify: it's called the GE Spacemaker II and it one of the few microwaves that is approximately 12½" deep — perfect for mounting under a wall cabinet, while still leaving usable working space below it.

Be careful of the outlet location — the electrical plug for the microwave is about an inch thick and will add to the overall depth.

As we move further into the future, you're going to see more of the microwaves combined into a secondary oven. We already have them now — speed ovens which combine microwave, convection, and grilling. If your kitchen is small, but you really want double-ovens and a microwave, this may be a viable option.

What's the best height for a microwave?

I usually suggest the bottom of the unit should be at the same height as the bent elbow of the most frequent user. That is, between 36"–42" off the floor.

Our designs often don't allow us that luxury (another way of saying that there's not enough space.) The microwave mounted in a tall 24" deep cabinet above an oven often is usually too high for anyone 5'4" and under.

This is the GE microwave built into a hutch. The bottom of the micro is 56" — a bit high for someone under 5'3".

Angled Microwave? Avoid designing your microwave next to an angled corner—corners are 12" deep with the door; the smallest microwave is 12½"—the corner cabinet door won't open and/or the microwave door will bind on the cabinet door next to it. (Unless you have a wide filler or spacer between them.)

When to install a microwave over a cook top or wall oven

Consider it in your design when:

- Kitchen space is tight and installing the microwave on a wall cabinet shelf will eliminate the few cabinets you have for dishes.

- There are only adults in the home.
- The range or cook top is a standard electric or induction.
- The microwave front is glass and metal, not plastic. The plastic tends to burn after a few years.

Don't consider it in your design when:
- Your range is a "pro" range with high–heat burners
- Small children are in the family. (They tend to rest hands and legs on cook top burners to reach the microwave.)
- You cook with big stock pots (not enough room on back burners for stirring).
- You're less than 5'2" (we lose some strength in our arms as soon as we raise our elbows above shoulders. Lifting a steaming bowl of soup out of the microwave could be dangerous. I'll talk about this a bit later on).

A quick thought on warming drawers: In this area of California, we're not permitted to place receptacle outlets behind appliances—they must be placed in an accessible location. This can be a challenge for the oven towers with the double oven and warming drawer combination. If placed between a refrigerator and a wall, you'll need to figure out alternate access. When it happened to me, luckily the wall was a walk–in pantry, so we could build an access panel for the warming drawer receptacle inside the pantry.

Ovens
Standard, convection, steam, and speed

The best height for a separate wall oven

Oven placement is a common error for a newbie designer. Stories abound of tall designers and architects placing ovens so high that the shorter client can't use them.

The entire reason for separating the oven from the cook top is for proper ergonomic height for the cook. Of course, this doesn't always happen. As more appliances come onto the market, the oven often has to fight for space with the microwave, the speed–oven and even the cappuccino maker.

Design the oven too high and you risk burning your arms on the oven door. Design it too low or the same height as a regular range, and you'll risk wondering why you spent the extra $500.00–$1,000.00 more to split the oven and cook top in the first place.

The ideal height for the main cook is determined by a simple test: Put your arms at your sides. Now raise your forearms keeping your elbows at your sides as if you were holding a platter. There. Approximately 6" below your elbow should be the bottom of the oven, or approximately 30"–40" off the floor.

The "soup test" of double oven placement

Not every kitchen lends itself to a separate cook top and oven design. My rule of thumb has been any kitchen less than 150 sq. ft. isn't spacious enough, but it always depends on the room configuration, the design, and the openings. Most of us compromise on both heights, so that one is a little low, and the other is slightly too high for at least one member of the family.

Here's how to get the best height — the higher of the two appliances is typically the microwave. If it's the second of the double ovens, it's also the more used of the two because it's easier to see inside when food is cooking.

In the planning stages, imagine lifting a bowl of soup into that top oven. As soon as you have to shrug your shoulders up and/or lift your elbows above your shoulders, the placement is too high — you lose strength in your arms, plus the steaming, bubbling liquid is now dangerously close to your face.

Lower the top unit so the top oven shelf is at shoulder height. If it's much higher than that, it's time to rethink both the layout and your appliances.

Yes, I understand. Many of you could mention kitchens where you've seen this, but it isn't considered optimal design.

Door openings affect oven height and placement

Microwaves are hinged on the left and swing open to the left — so design-ing them next to a wall that is on the right hand side of the microwave cramps movement, especially if the microwave is built into a tall cabinet. If this is your design, it can be helpful to add some nearby counter ("landing space") nearby, or selecting a microwave/convection oven with a door that swings down like an oven.

Speed–cook ovens are a combination of microwave, convection, and grill. They're also hinged like ovens and open the same way. That "hinge–down" position of a potentially heated door is something that everyone should think about during the design stage — what are the heights of the people who will use it the most?

Space is tight?
Replace your second oven and microwave with a speed–cook oven

One of the challenges, especially in older homes, is that by the time we add all the appliances — the dishwasher, the main and prep sinks, the refrigera-tor, the double ovens, cook top, and microwave — we're eying the oven cavities as possible storage places.

Speed–cook ovens (or speed ovens) are a smaller unit slight-ly larger than a microwave but smaller than a second oven. They operate as a microwave or convection oven or even a grill.

If you have to have a second oven which is seldom used, why don't you eliminate that second oven and microwave for a single speed oven? Speed ovens are energy efficient as there's no

If the island is large, consider raising a portion to 42" high — the extra height makes it easier to access the microwave and the raised counter makes a great place to lean against for a drink or two.

pre–heating required, and the convection ensures you can cook food in a fraction of the time. Now we can combine two appliances into one, have room to store things…and our chicken can be from oven to table in ½ hour.

Final thought—Extended warranties

As appliances become more futuristic with control touch sliders for cook top controls and touch screens on the ovens with databases of recipes, I'll leave you with this: consider extended warranties on all your new appliances if they're offered by your appliance store. Electronics are a, er, touchy element and can be affected by power surges or simple manufacturing details. I've seen more and more of the high–end units requiring maintenance sooner than I'd like, and having the extended warranties for these new designs could prove to be a very worthwhile investment in the long run.

CHAPTER 14

MOPPING UP FLOOR MISTAKES

Many people regard flooring for the looks first, forgetting about the function, installation, and design elements too late, especially if the floor is the only item in the kitchen to be replaced.

In this chapter, you'll get the designer inside view of what we look for when designing with the various kitchen floorings — wood, vinyl, linoleum, laminates, tile, and stone. We'll look at what to watch for with the materials and how they wear over the long term, as well as the key details you should think of before making your final choices.

What a designer sees in flooring

These are the factors on the mental check list:

1) **Is it slip resistant?** There are a lot of liquids and ingredients spilled on the floor of a busy kitchen — from dishes loaded and unloaded at the dishwasher to the flour that spills off the counter. For a single person, it might be fine. For a busy family of 5, the wrong flooring choice could turn into a skating disaster.

2) **Is it easy to clean?** Will it show dirt? Are there crevices or special care requirements down the road? I'm not trying to get out of cleaning, but I'm a survivor of the decade when white floors were in and all we did was

complain about how much work they were to keep clean. For busy families, I tend to think in warm, mottled hues rather than modern whites.

3) **What is the width of the flooring and how will it fit in the room?** Vinyl and linoleums are made in certain sizes. The last thing you want is a seam down the middle of your floor. No matter how wonderful your floor installer, seams don't wear well over the long term without more care.

4) **Is it durable?** Porcelain tile is more impact–resistant and durable than ceramic tile. Solid wood flooring which is laid in place can be repaired. Pre–finished wood floors have a special finish that can be quite rugged.

5) **Where is the house located?** Two of the worst enemies for flooring are water and sand. Are you in an area that receives plenty of rain or snow? Or on the beach where the kids track in sand? Either one of those will completely ruin a wood or laminate floor over time. Think about what is being tracked into the home and if there's an exterior entry into the kitchen.

6) **What is the lifestyle of the homeowner?** If Junior is on the soccer team and forgets to take his cleats off, you bet you don't want to install wood flooring in the kitchen (unless he can be trained). Are there animals already digging for traction in a race around the island? Will the window reflection in your high–gloss floor illuminate every streak and dust mote?

Test drive your floors: Purchase or order a sample of the flooring you like. Toss some potting soil on it and rub it in — see how much it shows and how easy it is to clean. Let the cat sleep on it. Place it in front of a window or door and see if you can see flaws. Drag a chair leg over it.* What you're looking for is not only how the flooring will stand up to every day use, but also your level of comfort about how the flooring wears before you buy.

* *Please don't use a showroom's sample — it's not fair to return a damaged sample. Look into buying samples of your own.*

Select the right flooring for your lifestyle

Soft floorings, such as vinyl, linoleum, and standard woods are:
- kinder to those with leg, feet, and back challenges than hard surfaces.
- quiet (with less chance of breakage) than harder surfaces when you drop something.
- a gentler surface for unsteady infants and toddlers to land on.

Hard floorings, such as tile and concrete are:
- resistant to paws and claws but don't provide much grip for claws. A dog or cat racing around is likely to slide.
- resistant to stronger cleaning products.
- Less likely to damage from sharp objects.

Replacing the floor but not cabinets and counters?

Here's the discussion from Chapter 12 on dishwashers and new flooring that I promised to expand on. In many 1970s and earlier homes, the dishwasher was an afterthought. The original floors were once a ⅛" layer (or two) of linoleum. So you decide you hate linoleum and the floor must go. Wood flooring is your dream, and a few months later, it's installed.

You've forgotten one detail.

Your dishwasher no longer fits under your counter.

It doesn't matter whether you installed the flooring up to the dishwasher or pulled the dishwasher so you could install the flooring underneath it — either way, you might run into trouble.

With the first scenario, if there's a problem with the dishwasher down the road,

The integrated dishwashers with the cabinet panels sometimes have a "sweep" toe kick (the recessed piece below the bottom dish drawer).

there's no way to remove it without damaging the floor or removing the countertop.

With the second scenario, if you're raising an already tight dishwasher an extra ⅜"–¾" due to your new floor installation, will the dishwasher still fit under the counter?

When I wrote a blog post on this a couple of years ago, it became my most popular post. Unfortunately, here's how people usually find it on my website — by searching for "dishwasher doesn't fit under counter" and "how do I get the dishwasher out without damaging the floor?"

Don't be like the online searchers. Check first.

How to check the appliance adjustment height

Before you decide on your flooring for your partial remodel, check how tight the dishwasher is to the underside of the counter. Some counter heights are also lower than the standard 34 ½" of height to the underside of the counter.

Remove the footplate and look at the adjustable legs. Is the top of the dishwasher is already as tight to the counter as it can go, and you can't lower the legs any further?

If so, you may have to either stick with the same existing style/thickness of flooring, or wait until you can afford to replace the cabinets and counters.

Sometimes, we have to work with what we have. I'd just hate for you to get your nice new floor in and discover this sad fact afterwards.

On the bright side: there's your excuse for those of you wanting or needing a new dishwasher/floor/counter/kitchen. "Honey? We can't replace the floor without new cabinets; the dishwasher won't fit."

Don't forget how the height of new flooring will affect new cabinets under a soffit or header

Every so often a homeowner will decide on a new wood or thick tile floor in the kitchen when the original flooring was a thin vinyl, and completely forget that this affects the height of tall pantry cabinet or a refrigerator cabinet under a soffit.

Measure your existing floor...and don't forget to
subtract the height of the new floor.

Floor Thickness Tip

An easy way to check existing flooring thickness — if your home has forced
air floor vents, remove the register cover. The edges will not only reveal
the floor thickness, it might also reveal how thick your subfloor is and if
there is more than one layer.

Those of you with wall registers or radiators might have to peel back
a seam or check in a corner of the kitchen or check the flooring at the
door transitions where you might be able to remove the transition at the
doorway.

Install the floor under the appliances

These appliances can be anything from dishwashers, ranges, icemakers,
trash compactors, and all refrigerators, whether they're full-size, beverage
centers, refrigerator drawers, or wine captain/coolers.

As mentioned in our dishwasher example, flooring should be installed
under the appliances. If the appliance ever needs repair, lifting the appliance
out from under a counter or under a wall cabinet will be almost impossible
if the appliance is tightly built in. The options then become lifting up the
counter to get additional height (not eager to try this when there's a half-ton
of marble involved), removing the wall cabinet above, or damaging the
floor as the appliance is wrested from its hole.

Do yourself a favor: ensure the flooring height under your appliances
will be the same height as the rest of the flooring in the room. I've seen
people install a sheet of plywood under the dishwasher instead of the
flooring to save a few dollars. I might argue that it's not the best idea under
appliances with potential water issues since I've seen how much plywood
swells when there's a major leak. Spend the extra money on the same
flooring under the appliances as well.

Pay attention to the flooring transitions

Flooring transitions are just that — the place where the flooring changes, say from the living room carpet to the wood floor in the hall. Most transitions are at doorways, although some can be at the front entry to the home.

Like the flooring and appliance scenario, you have to pay attention to the thickness of both floors. If there's a slight difference in height between the two, it can pose a tripping hazard, unless a strip to smooth the transition is installed between the two levels. Too much of a difference in levels and it forms a trip hazard. The transition strips can be as attractive as a wood strip between the two surfaces, or as standard as a silver strip between your carpet and vinyl. The strip not only minimizes tripping hazards, it also prevents sections of the floor from lifting. It's nothing that you need to spend a great deal of time thinking about — unless your two floors are radically different in height, or you hate the look of a standard metal or plastic transition.

My favorite tip for tile and carpet transitions

Schluter®-SCHIENE
metal flooring transition

One of the challenges of a transition between a hard surface and a soft surface in a traffic area is damage to the edge of the hard surface, particularly when you're moving large or heavy pieces of furniture in and out.

If your kitchen will have tile in the kitchen transitioning into carpeting at either the doorway or between an open kitchen and family room where a vacuum head could catch the edge just so, or a sofa dragged between the two surfaces could cause all sorts of chips and cracks, consider a metal transition piece called Schluter®-Schiene (www.schluter.com) between the two materials. It's a simple concept — a metal edge that protects the edge of your tile. It comes in different colors, as well as different shapes depending on surface heights.

Use caution when replacing older vinyl flooring

If your floors are 1970s and earlier (like the old square 1950s tile which were everywhere), your existing vinyl flooring or vinyl floor tiles may contain asbestos. (It made the floors more durable. No one knew at the time it'd be at the expense of our health.)

Another sign is if you remove a first layer of flooring and discover a sheet of plywood or other material over a lower layer of vinyl or vinyl tiles. Or you discover two or three layers of flooring.

Asbestos in the flooring isn't a concern until you attempt to remove the flooring — and you shouldn't. If it's pulled up or broken up, it frees the asbestos particles into the air — the last thing you want to do. Some recommend sealing the flooring (if it isn't cracked or peeling) or contacting an asbestos abatement company.

Visit your state or provincial environmental agencies for their rules or regulations (federal regulations trump state agencies in the U.S.) on how you should handle the flooring before you start your demolition.

Heated flooring — yes or no?

Heated flooring is achieved in two ways — with piping which runs under your flooring, usually in a newer home with concrete slab foundation, or in a thin sheet which is installed between the sub-floor and the underside of your flooring.

I hate to sound like a broken record, but each manufacturer will let you know what types of floorings work best over this heating element.

What I can tell you is that I like using it under tile, but a bit wary of using it under vinyl and wood — wood especially. One of the reasons I don't use it under vinyl is because the heat could dry out the material over time. We use vinyl because it's easy care and affordable but most aren't meant to be combined with heat.

This also applies to wood. Wood flooring expands and contracts depending on the moisture in the air. If there's a lot of moisture, the wood may swell and cup between boards. (Cupping is exactly that — the boards push against each other to form a "u" shape, so it looks like a miniature sea.) What the heated floor will do is the opposite — dry out your boards so they shrink and gaps form between them. I might argue on the side of caution not to use them. (Woods are also far warmer on the feet than tile.)

Where heated floors work best is with tiles in both stone and man-made.

When a kitchen is in full swing, with the ranges and all the appliances running, it can be the warmest room in the home. However, having a heated floor for colder climates can be the best feeling in the world when you get up in the icy dark to make your coffee in the morning.

CHAPTER 15

LIGHTING TIPS TO KEEP YOU ON TRACK

My father was fond of saying, "If factories had been lit the same way kitchens were, safety officials would have shut them down for insufficient lighting."

Luckily for us, lighting in the kitchen is better now than it was in the late 1970s and 1980s. With today's new lighting and the growing acceptance of fluorescents and LEDs (light emitting diodes), it's more important than ever to cover some easy tips on lighting and show you some tips on basic color temperature of lighting and how to avoid "muddying" kitchen colors.

This chapter isn't meant to be the definitive answers or even show you the latest in lighting — there are entire books devoted to lighting and techniques. In fact, if your kitchen plans are large scale or elaborate, with multi-level ceiling treatments and multi-use areas (nooks, bars, television stations), I strongly urge you to hire a lighting designer — the difference in your lighting will be well worth it.

In this chapter, I want to cover the same questions that my clients have asked me over the years — not only details such as height of hanging pendants — but also highlight the areas we need to watch for when planning a lighting design for the kitchen.

Before we do that, let's first tackle where your money goes.

The many layers of lighting (low to high):

Over the years, the single bulb in the middle of the ceiling has given way to increased general room lighting, task lighting for cooking and prepping areas, and accent lighting to highlight cabinets or wash the walls and ceiling in lights.

Why would we add all these layers? Because lighting sets the mood, and there are many factors that affect it — the hour of the day, the time of year, the way the house is situated, the number of windows — all of these play a part into the final plan.

It's a reason why I prefer multi-switching of lights in a kitchen, even if the kitchen is only a tight galley. We don't need every light in the kitchen on at once. We might want only an accent light to highlight our path to the refrigerator if we're watching movies, or all the lights switched on when the kitchen is full of people during the dark winter evenings.

Starting with the basics, here's how we'd layer according to budget. If your budget is:

Basic

Consider a ceiling-mounted fixture or two which doesn't require recessing into the ceiling. This could be a globe or a glass shade or a single pendant chandelier. This is most cost-effective because it requires the least amount of labor and material costs for lighting, wall and ceiling repairs, and paint.

Add hardwired under cabinet lighting

(Hardwired means it's directly wired and doesn't need to be plugged into your outlets but it also needs a switch.) Fluorescent gives the most light spread. Budget-friendly option includes a toggle switch attached to the light and a plug-in option vs. the more expensive hardwire. More expensive items are low-voltage lights, which can be hotter and require a transformer, LED strip lighting, and Xenon.

Add low-voltage lighting

This would be instead of can lighting or decorative general lighting pendants. Be aware that most low-voltage lighting, from LED to halogens, require a transformer (roughly the size of a shoebox or smaller) installed somewhere in the kitchen. Check your local codes for which ones you're allowed to use.

Add a decorative light for general lighting

These include anything from pendants to large scale designer pieces composed of multi-lights. Can vary in cost from under $100.00 to $1,000.00 and more. Still, it's cheaper than the next option.

Add recessed can lighting

More of your ceiling has to be repaired (unless the electrician can work from the attic), which will also mean painting. Cheapest bulbs of all are incandescent, but over time you'll pay more in energy bills. LED and fluorescent are 3-4 times more than the initial cost of incandescent, but you'll recoup the money in energy savings over time.

Add pendant lights

Single pendants are less expensive in both materials and labor costs than cable systems where the lighting is suspended from an exposed cable run across the entire length of the room.

Add up-lighting

This is lighting placed on top of your cabinets or built into a ceiling treatment. For safety's sake, I tend to avoid heat-emitters such as halogen but ambient up-lighting tends to be a must in higher-end design.

Add wall sconces

Most standard kitchens don't have room — these are for sizeable kitchens (although I have added them in the nook/breakfast area. It all depends on your design). Again, this is another area where the walls need opening up for wiring, which requires repair and painting. This is another way to add yet more ambient light to the kitchen.

Check your local energy codes: In California, for example, we need to follow the Title 24 Energy Code, which aims at better energy usage by avoiding 100% low-efficacy lighting. See *www.energy.ca.gov/title24/2008standards* for details.

In the Can — avoiding the five biggest mistakes of recessed can lights

Unfortunately, many people pay more attention to cost than function and in the case of can lighting, cheapest is not the best — not for long–term, not for the lighting, and not for how it'll work in the kitchen.

I'm not going to delve into the pros and cons of flood and spot lighting, other than to mention pay attention to how high the bulb sits within the housing — this can really affect the light spread.

Whether the lighting is incandescent, fluorescent, or anything else, recessed can lighting or recessed pot lighting is a down light system. With the exception of fluorescent, which spreads the light, most forms of lighting will be behind your head, which will cast shadows exactly where you don't need them. This is one of the reasons I rarely place a single light over the range and sink. I typically design two cans, one on each side of the sink and range, so that the light spread of both dissipates the shadow. *Here are some other considerations:*

a) **Light Spread:** There are two areas you want to think about — The first is blocking the light to the counter by positioning lights behind your head and casting a shadow. The second is to placing the lights so close to the wall and pantry cabinets that they creates a "hot spot" or high degree of reflective light on the cabinets which is also not ideal.

This is a 108" (9 foot) ceiling. Even in black and white, see how the lights placed too close over the refrigerator create that hot spot of light on the cabinet?

b) **Kitchen lighting is not the same as other room lighting.** While some may argue about symmetry in a room, the best position to install the can lights is over the counter and working areas where you need them. That sets a recessed can approximately 18"–24" from the walls (because wall cabinets have a typical 2"–4" crown which set their overall depth to 14"–16" from the walls.) For tall pantries, ovens and refrigerators that are 24"–30" deep, allow at least 8" from the crown molding edge.

c) **Avoiding ceiling acne.** You might know this one: when the ceiling is peppered with dozens of can lights? Not the most attractive solution and with incandescent lighting, a waste of energy. There are as many different bulbs for lighting levels as there are cabinet choices (not quite, but close). If you have that dilemma, hiring a lighting expert for a couple hours might be a very good solution.

d) **Some systems work better with dimmers than others.** Sometimes we don't need full power in the kitchen — we want a softer light so it doesn't spill into other rooms when we're entertaining or watching a movie. While incandescent and LED can be dimmed, I've found that fluorescents don't dim well, even with the best dimmer system. The reason is that when the power is lowered on a fluorescent, it simply turns off, so there is no gradual smooth transition from low to bright — more of a jerky motion. So, until they figure out a way to change this, I don't really see a solution in the foreseeable future.

e) **Be safe.** As with walls, take care in discovering what is hidden behind the ceiling sheet rock or plaster before you cut. There can be existing wiring or plumbing or even gas lines buried inside, which is easier to check in a single–story home than a multi–story. Simply cutting where you want without care could be dangerous.

**Regular incandescent bulbs are being phased out
in favor of high energy efficient bulbs.**
The Energy Independence and Security Act of 2007 set the
standards for manufacturers to create better energy–efficient
light bulbs by 2012. This law will require light bulbs to use 25–30

percent less power than incandescent bulbs we currently use. It doesn't mean that your incandescent bulbs are going away (except in California by 2018), but that they will be more energy-efficient.

Will your cabinets extend to the ceiling?

Sometimes, the cabinetry design has only a small trim next to the ceiling. *If the doors extend almost to the ceiling, you might have a problem opening the doors if:*

- The ceiling light fixture is thicker than the space between the top of the door and the ceiling
- The cabinets extend to the ceiling without a trim at all, and the recessed can light are placed too close to the cabinets. This happens most in contemporary design — the recessed can isn't flush — the trim you see on the light protrudes down ever-so-slightly.

The solution is to check the height and placement of your lights. In the case of the can lighting, check the height and construction of the cabinets. For frameless doors, some cabinets lower the doors ⅛" down from the top of the cabinet case; for others, they might suggest installing a small piece of molding between the top of the cabinets and the ceiling.

Pendant lighting

Out of all the questions I get asked, the number one question is, "What height do I hang the pendant lights?"

It'd sure be nice if there was a strong guideline: "Never hang your light any further than…"

For standard 8' high ceilings, it's a balancing act and the answer depends on many factors:

- The height of the cooks — it's no use having pendant lighting if the kitchen layout dictates that you'll weave and bob to see past the lights to your guests' faces. Or knock yourself out cold every time you want to work on the counter underneath them.
- The height of pendants is affected by the height of the counters.

- Is the scale of the pendants in proportion with the room? Are they meant to be a visual element or not?
- If the pendants are placed on a peninsula — the open counter section of a u–shaped kitchen layout — will they obstruct any openings of nearby wall cabinets?
- Will you be reading, eating, socializing, or cooking — or all of them? How much light do you feel you need? The shade, the bulb placement, and especially the color can make all the difference to the lighting levels. If you don't know any of these, consider a dimmer switch for greater lighting control.

With an 96" high (8 foot) ceiling and a standard 36" high counter, these thin 2½" diameter pendant lights are installed at 66"off the finished floor. The left pendant is just out of reach of that wall cabinet door on the left.

Here's my typical room of thumb. In an 8 foot ceiling, I keep the pendants small–to–mid size (3"–6" diameter). They look best when the bottom of the pendant is approximately 63"–66" off the finished floor. I also space them 30"–36" apart, or at least 6"–12" away from a cook top and an absolute minimum of 12" away from the counter edge.

If you're placing your pendants over an island and the island is only 24" deep, I might recommend against pendant lighting, as there would be no good way of installing a pendant without someone's head hitting it during food preparation.

Kelly's "Rolling Pin" method of setting pendants.
Stand at any kitchen counter. Imagine rolling out a pie crust. If you don't bake, pretend to make a sandwich instead. The distance you lean forward is the distance before you'll hit your head on the pendant. Let's avoid that. Apply that depth to every end of the island that could be used for baking or prep work.

It's not even a good idea with a 36" deep island, especially for a tall cook. When he or she leans over to cook, there's a good chance of collision between head and light.

Don't forget the shade color affects the light

We order a lot of lights from catalogues and online, which is a shame, because we really need to see how the glass changes color when the light is both on and off.

I once had a glass shade that showed as caramel online, but when we took it out of the box, it was almost purple — the photo hadn't shown it with light switched off. This dark glass shade was a bit of an eye–opener for both the client and I but thankfully still worked well in the color scheme.

I'm telling you so you'll know what to watch for. In addition, be cautious of pendants with wide shades or overly large–scale pendants in a small space — they'll not only dominate the room, but they'll also act as dividers during conversations.

A common mistake to avoid with pendant lights on a peninsula

A peninsula is simply an island that is attached to a wall of cabinets. In your design, are there any adjacent wall cabinets where the door could swing into the pendant?

If so, then the cabinet should either be an open shelf, or the pendant should be moved out of reach of the door.

What if my ceilings are higher than 8 feet?

Then you have a little more luxury of placing the pendant height, but you also have to watch the scale of the light in proportion to the room. Tiny spot light pendants will look undersized in a larger room with a higher ceiling. Your pendants can be larger.

Higher ceilings allow for higher pendant heights. Here's a 108" high ceiling with the pendants at 76" off the floor.

Select the right color of lighting

Our ordinary light bulbs cast a warm, reddish glow. Fluorescent lights vary from very cold light to very warm light. LED comes in a variety of colors.

We measure them all with Kelvin scale, used to describe a light's color temperature in degrees ranging from 1,000–10,000. The higher the number means the bluer and cooler the color. For purposes of our discussion, kitchen lighting varies between 2,700–4,100 degrees Kelvin. (There could be some regional variations.) An ordinary light bulb is around 2,800 Kelvin, fluorescents vary from warm (2,700) to cool (8,000), and LEDs range from warm to cool (3,000–6,000). You never used to hear of it in basic kitchen design, until fluorescent lighting returned and all the CFL (compact fluorescent lights) were graded on this scale.

So why is it important? Because the wrong color of light "muddies" your room colors.

If you have a contemporary kitchen filled with platinum grays and royal blues, adding warm lighting in the 2,500–3,000 Kelvin range will muddy the colors.

If you have a warm, traditional kitchen filled with creams and woods, adding cool lighting will take away the warmth of the colors.

Different colors of light bulbs affect your overall kitchen design

In our showroom, we have two under cabinet fluorescent lights, one on each side of a display cook top. One is a warm 2,700 degrees Kelvin, the other a cool 4,000 degrees Kelvin. The wall is painted a soft wheat color. The paint turns a yellowish gray under the cool light, and looks warm and inviting under warm light. Guess which one people like the best? The warm. But if the kitchen walls had been painted platinum grey, the choice might have changed. The gray would look taupe–colored under the warm white fluorescent and more to its true color under the cool white.

Fluorescent Lighting Tip: Most fluorescent fixtures on the home market are shipped out with cool fluorescents, not warm.

What you should know about under cabinet lighting

Light spreads downwards, over the backsplash, and onto the counter. If you want good task lighting, install the lights mounted on the underside of the wall cabinets closer to the front of the cabinets (and understand there will be some sort of molding to hide the wiring under the cabinet. Some jurisdictions allow it; some don't). If you want a backsplash "wash", install the under cabinet lights closer to the wall.

Fluorescent lighting spreads more evenly, which makes it a better choice for a lighting wash on the backsplash, but if you space the ballasts too far apart, there will be a shadow cast onto the splash. Keep them installed tightly together in a line along the underside of your cabinets.

LED lighting, xenon, and halogen are mainly "spot" lights in that they'll cast individual pools of light onto the counter, the splash or both. LED are the newest and coolest, but be aware that the color consistency between the LEDs isn't consistent in some brands, so that the color might be warm and inviting for one, and cool and blue for another. Halogens are a very warm light and not necessarily the most energy efficient.

Some final tips

We're in for some exciting changes in lighting and it's also one area most people ignore. If there's one thing I've learned in lighting, it's that the most inexpensive lighting rarely lasts long.

General lighting can be a good start, but if you want your kitchen to have real sparkle, the lighting plan should be a combination of the three types of lighting: general (pendant/recessed), task (counter), and ambient (up–lighting/sconces) lighting. To see this for yourself, study kitchen photos. The more expensive kitchens always have a combination of the three.

CHAPTER 16

OPEN AND SHUT CASES — DOORS AND WINDOWS

Most kitchen designs don't account for doors, windows, or trims — casings, baseboards, chair rail, wainscoting, and crown molding — which can cause delays in installation, and ruin some important design elements.

This chapter won't cover all the different styles of trims, doors or windows, but instead will focus on how they affect the overall design and function of the kitchen.

The rule for specifying correct interior door swings

One of the biggest mistakes of door ordering is mistakes on door swings. We're not talking cabinets, we're talking about the doors and entries into your kitchen. If you're the one who'll be ordering your interior doors and the person at the lumberyard/supply store/door place asks you: "Which way do you want the door to swing?" here's a simple way to figure it out.

Stand outside the room facing the door. Which side is the hinge on? Is it the right? Does the door swing in? Then it's a right–hand in–swing. Left? It's a left hand in–swing. **1** [see next page.]

- All doors for rooms swing into the room, for bedrooms or any rooms one enters from a hallway (in–swing).
- Let's say you have two rooms together, say the kitchen and dining room and the door swings into the dining room. Doors are config-ured to the room you're in, so this one is up to you. It could either

be called a dining room door, in which case it's an in–swing, but if you call it a kitchen door, then it'll be called an out–swing. Whatever you do, decide which room you'll label the door as, and don't change your mind.

- Closet doors swing outward and away from the closet.
- Kitchen interior doors seem to swing depending on layout, and in older homes, sometimes swung both ways. Or, if you're lucky, you may have pocket doors and won't have to worry about it.

Not everyone uses this method, but it's helped me keep the orders straight over the years. If you're still not sure, bring the floor plan with you.

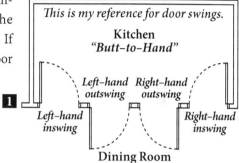

This is my reference for door swings.

Kitchen
"Butt–to–Hand"

Left-hand outswing *Right-hand outswing*

Left-hand inswing *Right-hand inswing*

Dining Room

Interior doors — solid or hollow?

The definition is pretty straight forward. Hollow doors have some interior bracing but they really do have a cavity between the panels. Solid core is as it sounds — we're now just talking the core, which will account for solid–core price differences.

If the budget is tight, and noise isn't an issue, buy a hollow door. This may come into play if you have a lot of doors that have to be replaced in your home. If you want a better noise barrier that is more impact resistant, select solid–core doors.

With a solid wood, the type of wood species will add extra dollars. Painting the door? Consider a less expensive paint-grade solid–core. Both are still more expensive than a hollow–core, but we might be talking $40.00–$200.00 at the most.

Honestly, if it's just one door — say between the dining room and kitchen, or the living room and kitchen, I might suggest solid core. (Especially if there is a speedy toddler and a tricycle…)

Can you reach it?
Three questions you need to ask yourself about kitchen windows.

Windows are one of the few finishing pieces where all modes of operation are mentioned from the exterior of the home. So, even if you have a gliding window and the right side opens from inside the kitchen, on the ordering copy the new window would state that the *left–side* is operable. This is the only part of the kitchen process where the ordering doesn't seem intuitive. I simply pretend I'm outside facing the window.

In terms of kitchen design, here's what a designer looks for:

a) How does your window open? Is it a casement window, where the panes swing to the outside like a door? Is it a single–or double–hung where the panes are stacked and you push one up or one down? Is it a slider where one or both side–by–side panels slide open?

b) What are you going to reach over in order to open the window? I hope your sink faucet doesn't have a large neck, or there aren't a lot of other fixtures to reach over.

c) How far away is the window from the front edge of the sink? We discussed this a bit with the angled sinks where the reach to the corner was almost 48" away. If I had two sliding windows that opened from the corner, I'd be hopping up on the counter to reach them and impaling my stomach on the faucet. Some of you might say this is not really an issue. Nothing is, unless the amount of time spent reaching the window means you end up never using it once the kitchen is finished.

My window's too high — can I lower it?

Many older homes once had wall faucets which made the sink window higher than the newer designs of today. Surprisingly, if you were already planning on replacing the sink window, it's not that expensive to lower the sill and order a taller window. It makes it easier for a shorter person to see out the window, it brings more light into the room, and it doesn't take long for a carpenter to reframe.

What you want to watch for is for "surprises" hidden below that window sill: old wall-mounted rough plumbing, the odd angled vent stack, not-to-code framing issues, and even wiring. Best to open up a patch of the wall before you order that window.

It is more expensive to raise the height of the window than it is to lower the sill as the framing above the window is usually structural, while the framing below the window isn't.

Don't forget to consider whether you can still get some of the old siding or stucco or whatever finish and color is currently on the exterior of the home.

Avoiding collisions — Crown molding and cabinetry, wainscoting, counters and windows

Every new designer forgets to account for door and window casing in their designs, particularly if they only specialize in cabinet design. In my area, older trim was smaller — a beveled 1¼". Then in the early 1990s, it expanded to a larger 2¼". In many older homes around the continent, the molding can sometimes be very elaborate and up to 5" wide or more.

Whatever the width, the correct way to install both casings is so the cabinets or other details don't overlap or cut into this trim. Now, I understand in a remodel where doors and windows aren't being changed, this isn't always possible, but here's what I look for.

a) What are the sizes of your casings and trims?

b) Will you be replacing them for something new?

c) Will this new trim be wider than your existing trim?

d) When designing the cabinets or any elements on a wall, I typically allow 3" of spacing per side for casings. I still check the actual casing sizing, but as I usually specify it, I have no one else to blame. If you can give some thought to what the moldings around your doors and windows will be as you start the cabinet design, you might save yourself some grief later.

e) Don't forget the window sill. Sometimes a window can be framed with casing, or it can be installed with a sill. The latter is a trim at the bottom of a window and it causes more grief than almost anything else in the kitchen. As we discussed in the plumbing section, it protrudes deeper than the wall, and can prohibit a faucet handle operation. It can also cause havoc if it's on an adjoining wall like the next photograph.

The left door of a double-door refrigerator would have taken some damage as it opened against that window sill. Even so, this existing refrigerator still needs some distance from the sill to pull the bottom freezer door out.

Windows to the counter and molding details

One of the details never successfully resolved — at least for me — is how to case a window when the window extends to the kitchen counter. Window trim or casing is not only used to decorate, it also seals the interior and exterior areas around those openings of the home.

Since the sink is usually installed in front of a window, potential water damage can occur where the wood or painted casings or jambs (the framing sides of the window) extend down to touch the (wet) counters. The cut portion of the trim (known as end-grain) acts like a wick when water or liquids reach it, often drawing the moisture up into the grain.

Here are a couple of options:

- If you want the wood or painted casing to extend down to the counter, add a bead of silicone around the edges where the casing and countertop meet.
- Build out the casing thickness from the wall if you're planning on having granite or tile backsplashes. Casing is ⅝" deep at the thickest point. Granites are ¾" thick; some tile and mudding can be nearly 1" thick. Do the two thicknesses match? If not, you'll need to build

out the casing to match by adding a strip of wood the same width as your molding, much like stacking blocks, but on the wall.

See how much this sill protrudes and how close the side casing is to the wall cabinet? It took some careful design to keep the plumbing fixtures and door swings clear.

- Some turn-of-the-century homes had only 24" from corner to doorway, a leftover from when counters were only 16"–18" deep. Instead of infringing on the door casing with a standard depth cabinet, consider installing a shallower depth pantry in the corner, or a shallower base cabinet. Whatever you do, don't install a refrigerator in the corner — it'll not only hide the casing but may obstruct entry into the kitchen!

A final tip

If your home is a contemporary style, or you're not planning on adding any trim, don't crowd your openings. That is, don't install all the cabinets right up to the doors, pass-through or windows. Leave some breathing room and even the tiniest of kitchens will feel less pinched as a result.

PART 4

PUTTING IT ALL TOGETHER — CASE STUDIES

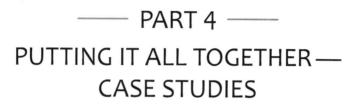

CHAPTER 17

PUTTING IT TOGETHER—
ONE KITCHEN, FOUR SCENARIOS

Remember our not–so–official survey at the beginning? Let's put it into action with the following scenarios.

The Reluctant Remodeler

While the remodel might have been something you planned, most likely something gave up the ghost in your kitchen or forced your hand. You don't want to do the work, but you need to know the best options, who to hire, even what questions to ask, so it can be fast, easy, and the value you need. [see page 8.]

Here is a plan of a late 1950s kitchen — slab plywood doors painted so many times, the doors stick in the frame. The counter was laminate and the floor was vinyl. **1** [see next page.]

So, o Reluctant Remodeler, let's say the cook top or oven is failing. The questions you want to ask yourself are:

"How long will I live in my home?"
- If you're planning only a couple of years, you have some options: find a new cook top and wall oven which fit into the existing cabinetry (this is important as ovens weren't as wide as they are today.
- If this is a long–term home (+/– ten years), then you might be consider an entire remodel down the road. Ask yourself whether you want to

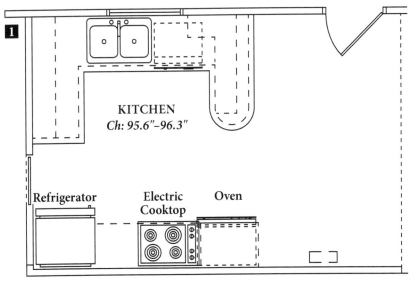

An original kitchen plan.

buy a narrower oven now (especially if you don't like the size), or buy an entire cabinet to fit the new oven, or hold off until you're ready. This is where the next question is important.

"What else needs to be replaced?"

- Perhaps the counter is sponge–y by the sink, a sure sign that either the counter or the sink cabinet has some water damage. Or the corner cabinet door is falling off. If the budget isn't there right now, consider hiring a contractor or handyman to perform basic repairs. Depending on the extent of water damage, you might be able to replace the counter with another laminate top (which involves removing and reinstalling the cook top and sink).

- If there are a lot of problems, be frank with yourself — patching a kitchen may be the only choice, but if it's truly past its time, you're only bandaging an artery. How many items will you buy knowing you'll spend your hard–earned money twice?

If I don't have the money to remodel right now, will I down the road?

- My sympathies if you're being pushed into this. You can either view it the same as repairing the roof or needing a new water heater — it's something that has to be done and you'll be glad once it's done. It all depends on you and how long you'll stay in the home.

The Cautious Planner

You've got some basic skills, and are willing to learn what you need, and maybe even a bit more. Will you DIY or not? You don't know yet, but you know enough that you want to research what's out there and avoid the most common mistakes. [see page 8.]

For you, the same questions apply for the amount of time you'll be living in the home, but you might be able to repair some of the details above.

"I might replace the floor"

- In this case, we have a sheet vinyl floor. Are you thinking of solid wood flooring or something that is thicker than the vinyl? If you're not replacing the counter or cabinetry, will the thickness of the new floor affect you being able to re-install the dishwasher or will it be too tight? Is there enough room under the interior doors to add a thicker floor?

"I might add a backsplash"

- Why not? If there's nothing there now but a small backsplash, you have the chance to add tile or wood or stone. What you'll want to pay attention to is the outlets and receptacles — if you can't move them, you'll have to design around them.

"I might change the lighting"

- Brighter light is a great way to eliminate the old and dingy air of a room. If you leave the ceiling electrical in the same place, it's easier to change the fixture than to re-wire, patch the ceiling and paint.
- The only caveat I would add is check to see that your electrical wiring is up to code or in good shape. If your circuit breakers pop (or even worse, you have fuses), I might suggest having an electrician check it out before you install that new higher-wattage fixture. I've seen a lot of ruined wired and charred ceiling joists from a too-heavy electrical load on old wiring.

"I might replace the counter."

- Some of the older cabinets were designed only to bear the weight of the lighter laminate counters (in those days, it was Formica). Are the cabinets strong enough to add a 1¼" stone counter? How about a ¾" counter?

- Are the cabinets made of individual boxes or are they built as a frame with all the shelves running through the entire space? Some cabinets fall apart when the counters are removed.

- Are your cabinets in good shape now? Don't spend a lot of money if your drawers are already falling apart. Eventually you'll need to replace them and the counters don't always transfer well because cabinet sizes have changed over the years.

The Enthusiastic DIY-er

You're skilled enough to gut the kitchen and stay away from structural changes. You're keen to get going on the physical work, but you know that there's a bit more to the design and planning stages for a kitchen than almost anything else in the home. [see page 8.]

For you, the Enthusiastic DIY–er, you'll do your homework, because if you're gutting the kitchen, chances are you might be doing it in stages. Or it might take so long that you change your mind in mid–stream and get caught on a design detail. It happens to all of us.

No one will oversee the big picture like you. So it's even more important to focus on the things you're about to accomplish, but let's go back to what I said in the beginning: "Not all products fit in every kitchen or with each other."

You're going to be concerned with the new layout. Let's say you take the wall measurements and the layout came back like so: **1** [see next page.]

Here's where you (and any one else considering a kitchen plan) ask these questions:

"Is it easy to cook my favorite meal?"

- I sometimes suggest to my clients to mentally cook a dish in their new layout — where will they go for pots or reach for the cookie sheets? Where are the pot holders? Does the prep area seem within reach?

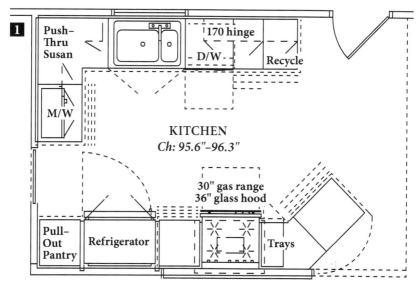

The previous kitchen revised and showing the open positions of all the drawers and doors

"How much do the appliances affect this layout?"

- This is the time to read the fine print in the appliance specifications. Is the pro range so deep that you can't get into the lazy susan beside it?

- Does the refrigerator door need a 135–degree door swing, and the plan places it next to a wall?

"Do any doors or drawers obstruct other openings, or bind them in any way?"

- Draw the door swings, the width and length of open appliance doors, and the swing of the interior and exterior doors in the room.

"Do any obstacles such as ceiling soffits or lighting pendants interfere with the cabinet placement?"

- I've heard plenty of tales over the years where someone forgot to measure the ceilings or forgot there were soffits above the existing cabinets — until the cabinets arrived.

"Does the durability and cleaning requirements fit with my lifestyle?"

- Some dark granites in front of windows show streaks — enough that one needs a wet wipe/dry wipe to remove the streaks — which isn't something you want to discover after a material is installed. Can you buy some samples and test them at home?

Working with your construction team

My clients are used to texting, email, social media, and cell phones to interact with our crew, but if your area isn't and your busy schedule interferes with meeting or contractor or trades on a timely basis, consider a communication center. Set it up wherever you set up your temporary kitchen or inside the entrance where your trades enter the home. It can be:

- *A chalkboard or corkboard, either on the wall, counter, or even an easel. You can pin or write the questions you have on the board before you leave in the morning and your contractor or trades can leave you a quick note in return.*
- *No room for the above? How about a hanging erase board with the pen on a string? Also consider a place to leave checks and invoices — perhaps a drawer or small cabinet. (Not recommended for new homes until lock-up when the walls, doors and windows are in.)*

The Informed Consumer

Unless you're a general contractor or an architect, it's doubtful you'll tackle structural changes or additions on your own. However, even if someone else is tackling the work, you still want to make the selections, communicate with the crew in a reasonable manner, and iron out any expectations in advance. Like the Cautious Planners, you're an overseer—any insider tips which help smooth out the design phase and will certainly pay off during construction. [see page 8.]

You're looking for a way to make conversation between you and your team smooth. Here are your additional questions:

"How the site will be cleaned? The trash removed?"

- It's the little details that calm us. Will site be broom-swept at the end of each day, or cleaned at the end of the week? Will there be a dumpster or a trailer?

"What are the working hours?"

- This is an important detail which can also include, "How quickly someone will get back to me if I have a question?" What can you expect from your team during the day?

"How will my concerns be addressed or challenges solved along the way?"

- Someone with experience will tell you exactly how, and might even share previous experiences. I was taught it's not simply how you design that makes you a professional; it's how you deal with challenges that seal the definition.
- Expect challenges, but don't be afraid to ask how they will be solved. Will there be change orders and what is the process?

Setting everything into motion

One of the details I discuss with my clients is that the course of building or remodeling seldom runs smoothly, no matter how hard we try. In re-modeling, we can order cabinets early even with a relocated wall because it's only one wall, not several. In new homes, we wait until the framing is up, and even then we double-check sheetrock/framing 2×4s to verify final measurements.

No matter how many times you measure, there might be a hidden dip in the floor under the cabinets or a hidden obstacle that forces a re-design. We once found a door framed in the wall of a very old home. One of my designer friends found the remains of an old tree. Those are two very odd scenarios, but they happen.

Most details usually require some minor tweaking and some details are simply beyond our control—anything from a tile out-of-stock even after multiple follow-ups to assure that it was in stock to unseen water damage in a wall from a leaky pipe to framing discrepancies between house plans and the final framing. Of course, when a project does run smoothly, everyone's happy.

Remember, it's all fixable, and what you're achieving will be beautiful. No one else will ever know what you originally picked.

Tips for living through a remodel (*as suggested by me*):

1. Set up a temporary kitchen in the dining room, living room, deck, or wherever an outlet is available. Have the refrigerator moved there along with a counter or cabinet or table set–up nearby with the microwave, and coffeepot. Move the plates, cutlery, and condiments there first.

2. Buy an electric or induction hotplate. This is a single or double element that can be plugged in and will allow some simple cooking, whether it's scrambling eggs or making chocolate sauce. (We can dream.)

3. Protect your entertainment equipment. Airborne dust wrecks havoc on electrical equipment like stereos and computers. Relocate if they're in the same room.

4. Is there a sink nearby? You're lucky if you have a laundry room sink or even a bathroom sink. Sometimes, we've plumbed for a temporary sink outside.

5. Plan for a message center near a phone so you can leave notes for family or the crew.

Tips for living through a remodel (*as suggested by clients*):

1. Disposable wipes and plastic containers may save your sanity. The wipes are helpful in the short term when there's no ready water source. Plastic containers keep the construction dust from getting into the plates and food.

2. Prepare casseroles or freezer food in advance. Package them in dinner sized portions because lasagna can dry out after repeated re–heating in the microwave.

3. Exchange dinner party favors with family and neighbors.

4. Drape sheets over bigger furniture before the plastic. Stops any particles from scratching the surface if the furniture gets moved.

5. Save the eating out for the latter part of the project. In the beginning, it's fun. Towards the end, it's nice to have someone else do the dishes and get away from it all.

The design steps from start to finish

Every person in this business has their own way of designing and ordering, but I thought you might like to see the steps I use for my own clients. Some of this will be repeated from earlier chapters.

In order, we start with:

1) **A rough idea of the material wish list.** We'll fine-tune as we go along, but in the beginning, it can be very helpful to know if my clients prefer a range, double ovens, or a big island with seating for three.

2) **The first fine-tuning of the design.** I usually invite my clients to mentally cook through the design. Where will the baking goods go? The pots? The waffle-maker and cookbooks?

3) **Select model numbers but don't buy the appliances, lighting, or plumbing fixtures.** We have the design. Now we see if the products fit. This is the time to see if the electrical panel can support the new appliances or if the sink and faucet will fit.

4) **The second fine-tuning.** We'll run with the tweaks of this second design — perhaps the refrigerator is deeper than planned, so the island needs to shrink. The appliances and plumbing fixtures all work, but we're stuck on the lighting. Fine. We'll come back to it.

5) **Decide on (and order) the cabinets and windows and doors.** Since most cabinets, doors and windows can take 4–6 weeks and some custom

orders can be from 8–20 weeks from the time of order, start "back–timing" or counting backwards from the week they need to be onsite to the time you order. For example, doors and windows should be onsite at start of construction with the cabinets arriving 3 weeks later. Thus a project starting mid–May needs the doors ordered at the beginning of April and the cabinets ordered mid–April.

6) **Decide on flooring.** Sometimes this is interchangeable with #5, simply because the flooring thickness affects the height of the cabinet installation.

7) **Get your bids for your sub–contractors.** Now that you have your design, get your prices for electrical and countertops. The benefit to doing so at this stage is that you'll know the layout details without having to make changes to your paperwork later. Last minute changes + multiple re–designs = mistakes on installation. Since they may have some insight into the final design details, this means:

8) **Fine–tune #3 for the layout.** Is the smaller sink bowl of your 1½ bowl sink on the right? Did you decide to upgrade your electrical panel or will it work as it is?

9) **Shop for lighting and backsplash.** I'm fond of saying that I often don't know the tile layout (or tile flooring) layout until I see the actual tile. Once we've fallen in love with both, guess what the next step is?

10) **Don't forget to take the items home to see how they look in your space.** If the existing lighting isn't good, place the materials by a kitchen window. Bring your samples to a lighting store to see how they look under various bulb colors. See how easy the samples are to clean.

11) **Fine–tune #4.** In a recent design, the client decided almost last–minute to switch from a 1½" thick counter to a 3"–thick design. This caused a domino design effect, as the faucet could only be installed in a 2³⁄₁₆"

thick deck, and the range had to be installed on a new tile platform to raise it to 37½" (the legs only raised the range to 36⅝" high). Pendant lights also had to be designed on the plans once we knew the actual shade dimensions.

12) **Handles, glass details, special treatments, casing and baseboard choices.** There is always one item in the choices that takes more thought than others. Some of these items should be discussed at the beginning, but usually end up at the end rush of final choices.

13) **Final fine-tune #5.** You can't double-check enough. This is the stage I fine that the 6" handle we selected won't fit on the 4" pull-out tray cabinet or that one of the entry doors needs to be adjusted so the casing around the door doesn't need to be cut to fit.

While we might focus on one element to act as a focal point — such as an island or a window — remember not to micro-focus. Use the five-foot rule — stand back five feet and view your choices again.

And remember — the goal is for you and your friends to say, "What a beautiful kitchen first, and then admire the individual details."

The construction steps from the start of construction to the end

Here's how your construction team might schedule the actual construction of your project. It may vary based on the project and has to allow time between trades for inspection:

a) demolition.

b) framer for walls, ceilings, skylights, doors and windows.

c) electrician for the wiring inside the walls, also called the rough electrical. Electricians expect two trips, one for "rough" and the other for "finished" — the lights and switch cover plates.

d) HVAC specialist for the installation of new rough heating and ducting.

e) plumber — who has two trips the same as the electrician.

f) insulation, sheetrock and texture.

g) cabinet install. If any wall cabinet extends down to the counter, you'll need to let the installer know he'll be making two trips as he'll have to wait until the counter is installed.

h) counter install. With stone tops, this can take anywhere from 5–10 business days from the time that they measure the cabinets on-site to fabrication and installation. We label this "down-time" because unless there are other areas to work in as appliances, backsplashes or finished electrical can't be completed until the counter is in.

i) backsplash installation — unless it was part of the counter.

j) painting. Some painters like to come in before the cabinets are in and touch up later; others think a touch up always shows and prefer to come in before the appliances but after everything else. I've seen both done well.

k) appliance installation.

l) final heating, electrical and plumbing — installing all the finish material.

m) cleaning crew.

n) Furniture placement and interior design.

o) Blinds and other coverings.

p) Celebrate!

There can be more items depending on the complexity of design. How long each stage takes depends on the materials, how many people are involved, and how custom they are. Sometimes engineering is involved prior to the start of construction, yet still affects the framing schedule, or co-ordination needs to happen between a kitchen addition and the landscape designers.

For those of you who aren't doing it yourself, you'll have some idea from your design team on timelines and orders, which may vary slightly depending on your project.

CHAPTER 18

CONGRATULATIONS, YOU'RE A PRO (OR AT LEAST, THINKING LIKE ONE!)

Obviously, there is so much to kitchen design that I might not provide something for everyone. As I was writing the book, ideas kept coming and coming until I was afraid you'd have a hefty door stop instead of a useful design book.

The evolution of kitchen design means that there are always new tips and techniques to discover, and hopefully the ones in this book should not only help you overcome some of the common and not–so–common problems, but save considerable unnecessary time and expense.

Before we end, I'd like to touch on a couple more details to make your life simpler after your kitchen project is finished and you're moved back in.

What happens after "Happily Ever After"?

In the haste for marketing and showing only the best and the shiniest, very little is discussed about what happens to the products over the long term, and what you should pay attention to regarding your family and lifestyle now.

Before you even use your new kitchen, know this: Grandma's cleaning methods and solutions aren't the best anymore. They're too harsh. The new finishes and new methods of manufacturing have complicated multiple–step finishes that don't interact well with common household products. The days of using full–strength products are gone.

For example, many cabinet manufacturers recommend mild soap and water rather than old-fashioned oils or soap which will merely sit on the surface creating hazy streaks until you clean them. Some glass and metal tile manufacturers shudder at the idea of abrasive cleansers.

You'll find the answers in the manufacturer's manuals supplied with your products, as well as online.

Whether you have a cleaning person, yourself, or a sulky teenager, discovering what the manufacturers recommend for cleaning before you start cooking might save you from the "oh no" during the first five minutes of use.

A binder is your friend

With all the complexities of design and multiple parts and pieces, compiling a binder with all the names and source of the materials you bought (and where) can be a real life-saver. If a part fails some months later, or you plan to add extra cabinets in the dining room to match the kitchen, you'll always know where all your information is, especially if you remember to include all the manuals, warranties, and design information.

Enjoy!

I sincerely hope you find the tips useful and they help you avoid most common (and not-so-common) kitchen design errors. If you'd like to find more tips, you can find me at my website, www.kellyskitchensync.com. I'd love to hear from you.

Good luck!

Made in the USA
Lexington, KY
20 July 2012